my WHEELCHAIR

MY JOURNEY OF GETTING BACK UP ON MY FEET

WAEL IBRAHIM

First published by Ultimate World Publishing 2022
Copyright © 2022 Wael Ibrahim

ISBN

Paperback: 978-1-922714-67-1
Ebook: 978-1-922714-68-8

Wael Ibrahim has asserted his rights under the Copyright, Designs and Patents Act 1988 to be identified as the author of this work. The information in this book is based on the author's experiences and opinions. The publisher specifically disclaims responsibility for any adverse consequences which may result from use of the information contained herein. Permission to use information has been sought by the author. Any breaches will be rectified in further editions of the book.

All rights reserved. No part of this publication may be reproduced, stored in or introduced into a retrieval system, or transmitted in any form, or by any means (electronic, mechanical, photocopying, recording or otherwise) without the prior written permission of the author. Any person who does any unauthorised act in relation to this publication may be liable to criminal prosecution and civil claims for damages. Enquiries should be made through the publisher.

Cover design: Ultimate World Publishing
Layout and typesetting: Ultimate World Publishing
Editor: Marinda Wilkinson

Ultimate World Publishing
Diamond Creek,
Victoria Australia 3089
www.writeabook.com.au

TESTIMONIALS

Wael Ibrahim needs to be commended for writing *My Wheelchair*. It makes for compelling reading because it is both personal and universal. Personal because it narrates the author's trials and tribulations in a way that is engaging and riveting. It is neither self-loathing nor self-laudatory. It is authentic and illuminating. This beautiful motivational book will have a profound impact on the hearts and minds of those who read it and reflect on it. It is this universality that is appealing.

The reader participates vicariously in the life of Wael Ibrahim. What I like particularly is that it is didactic and does not pontificate. The author's journey is both physical and spiritual. His trials made him reconnect with the purpose of life. His pointed reference to the Qur'an and to the prophetic tradition is a significant feature of this book.

My Wheelchair does not leave you despondent — in fact, it propels you to take ownership of your life, both through action and by surrendering yourself to the Creator. The lessons you glean from the life of Wael, the protagonist, are too numerous to mention. Suffice to say that it can be life-changing. On a personal level I felt invigorated and most importantly it reminded me about my purpose on this earth.

I thoroughly enjoyed reading this great piece. It wasn't pedantic or esoteric, and makes for easy reading because it is succinct and the issues outlined are pertinent.

It is evident that Wael wants you to begin your journey of healing. The two blank pages at the beginning is stylistically very creative. What he wants is that we should not be passive or adopt a victim mentality. What is needed is action, understanding the profound message of the Qur'an, and to embrace its finest exemplar our beloved Prophet Mohamed PBUH.

Edris Khamissa,
Consultant in Education and Human Development
www.edriskhamissa.com

Testimonials

Once again, Wael Ibrahim strikes very hard. But this time via the means of giving us a vivid example of his personal life and an experience of a whole year of physical and emotional pain. The way he handled and courageously faced his painful experience is a lesson for us all to live by.

My Wheelchair is a book where you get the necessary inspiration to convert your negatives into absolute hope of realistic positivity and uplifting of one's faith in Allah's Qadar (destiny).

Dr. Muhammad Salah,
Huda TV, Egypt

Thank you, brother Wael Ibrahim, for such a helpful book that connects personal life experiences with the ultimate purpose of our existence. And that is to continue worshipping God Almighty despite any difficulty we may face in life.

Thank you for using the Qur'an to establish the link between experience and purpose, in a very clear, simple and easy-to-understand manner.

Sheikh Fadel Soliman
Director of Bridges Foundation and
author of Coptic Christians before Muhammad PBUH

My Wheelchair

Wael Ibrahim's story is one that brings to light hope in the midst of darkness and hopelessness, triumph over difficulty, purpose after purposelessness, and the understanding that there is always a victorious rise after a fall. Compelling, relatable, powerful, and reflective, I can't help but feel empowered by his string of words as he brings me through his past and present experiences, filled with gems and wisdom that only experience can bring.

It's amazing how the power of the mind, heart, and soul can transform a person's life. Negatives turn into positives, and through his pain, he was able to transform and bring us this incredible book to help us get through our own life struggles. May it be a source of inspiration and strength for all and may it be a means of continuous reward for him, Aameen.

Shazrina Azman aka Mizznina
(Known as Mizz Nina – Malaysia)
Co-founder of Qalby App, Dops TV,
Min Qalby Foundation and
author of Light for the Lost Soul
https://beacons.page/qalbyapp
https://linktr.ee/MinQalbyFoundation
https://m.youtube.com/c/DOPStv

A few days ago, I was with one of our senior speakers who was describing his struggle with pain and various disturbing consequences of the slipped disc he developed in the last

Testimonials

few years. I was not sympathizing with him, only because it is an Islamic duty, but also because I experienced this struggle when I was in my late twenties and I understand how painful and disturbing that is.

When I came home in the evening and checked my WhatsApp messages, I found a message all the way from Australia, from my dear beloved and creative brother Wael Ibrahim. He was reminding me to write a few words about his new book titled *My Wheelchair* which he wrote to inspire others in a practical way on how to overcome their difficulties in life. Amazingly, his experience is similar to mine, but with harder struggle.

My dear brother Wael was really inspirational and creative in providing practical steps that can enable many people to overcome their struggles in life. I only wish he wrote this book before my own struggles, so I could have dealt with them in a more positive and effective way.

What motivated me more to keep reading his book was the smooth language that he used. In fact, you read it as if you are reading a fictional book by one of the famous writers. Needless to say, that the solutions he provided are strongly rooted in Qur'an and Sunnah, which marks this work as a key contribution in this field. May Allah reward him and aid him so he can enlighten us with more similar works.

Sheikh Haitham al-Haddad,
Jurist and judge for the Islamic Council of Europe

My Wheelchair

My Wheelchair by Wael Ibrahim is a highly inspirational read, from start to end. In fact, I was so inspired that I read it in one sitting. Most of all, it's a real-life account of his experiences, good and bad, and it's captivating. Wael's personal account will resonate with every reader because every reader has their own 'wheelchair' experience.

As a work colleague of Wael's, I've seen him battle through his health challenges on a daily basis. As I read the book, I continuously recalled his positive mindset while sitting in his wheelchair and going on with his work life as though all is well.

What I find the most appealing in the book is the positive tone in which it is written. Even the most challenging moment is adorned with hope. Hope is what we need to carry with us through every step of our lives. No matter what curve ball is thrown at us, hope will carry us through.

By sharing his real-life story, Wael Ibrahim is doing all of us a great service in showing us how to handle the most challenging situations in our lives.

This book is a must-read!

Sheikh Yusuf Parker,
Head of Religion, Australian Islamic College and
Imam and Principal, Alhidayah Centre, Western
Australia

Testimonials

When calamity strikes, it causes panic in most cases. People start thinking negatively while dealing with it. Then it strikes again. People start complaining to each other while dealing with it. Then it strikes for a third time. People begin to question the Mercy of the Almighty. Then it strikes for a fourth time. By now people feel so battered that they resort to all sorts of negative behaviors, making matters worse.

Brother Wael Ibrahim's personal story shows us that while we're all just humans, by processing calamity after calamity through strengthened faith and renewed determination, and never giving up, we actually end up achieving beyond our imaginations.

A very good read with great life lessons.

Mufti Ismail Menk,
Mufti of Zimbabwe

ACKNOWLEDGEMENTS

My sincere gratitude, love and respect to some individuals who have helped me greatly in finalizing this project. They are, **_Clarissa Miller_** and **_Aly Balagamwala_** for going through the hassle of proofreading and making sure that most errors are eliminated.

I'd like to also thank the talented **_Muhammad Ehtesham_** for the amazing book cover design which has caused a great deal of hype on social media platforms due to its creativity and beauty.

And proudly, I'd like to thank my sweetest daughter, **_Habiba Ibrahim_** for the funny yet meaningful illustrations that was inserted before each chapter.

And last but never the least, I'd like to thank all my family members and friends who supported me during this very painful stage in my life.
You know well who you are ☺

Love you all.

DEDICATION

To my beloved wife, Fatimah Ibrahim who walked with me throughout this painful journey just as she has promised to walk with me on the journey of life, through thick and thin.

CONTENTS

Introduction. 1
Chapter One: Comfort 3
Chapter Two: Comfort-less 23
Chapter Three: Emotional Battles. 37
Chapter Four: The Wait 55
Chapter Five: Pain to Gain 69
Chapter Six: Realistic Positivity 83
Chapter Seven: Contentment 95
Chapter Eight: Stretch 109
Chapter Nine: Losers Give Up,
　Winners Give Value 123
Chapter Ten: Inspire Others 135
Final Word 147
About The Author. 149

INTRODUCTION

There are two blank pages in the beginning of this book. This is why — they are **YOURS** to start drafting your own path to getting back on your feet.

Within these pages is my story, which was written to inspire you to get unstuck, break free from the shackles of your difficulties, and live a meaningful life. But at the end of the day, this is **MY** book and **MY** story. Right now, **YOU** are more important than anything else. So, I decided to leave these two pages in the beginning **BLANK** so that you can always remember to come back here, to the beginning, and plan the first few steps that will change your life.

It was a blank notepad that sparked the idea for *My Wheelchair*. This is how I decided to get back on my feet after nearly paralyzing myself and being unable to walk for more than nine months. However, I later realized that the pain, hardship, torture, sleepless nights, fear, and so on were all necessary for me to go through and live with the memories associated with them. And as a result of this experience, I was able to get back on my feet.

In the Qur'an, Allah SWT, God Almighty stated:

> *"Or do you think that you will enter Paradise while such [trial] has not yet come to you as came to those who passed on before you? They were touched by poverty and hardship and were shaken until [even their] messenger and those who believed with him said, 'When is the help of Allah?' Unquestionably, the help of Allah is near."*
> Qur'an 2:214

Many times, along the way, we will need to be shaken in order to **MOVE** something that will help us stabilize our situation. As a result, don't try to avoid the healing process. It's unpleasant, but it's occasionally essential.

Enjoy the journey.

Wael Ibrahim

Chapter One

COMFORT

Comfort

We all want some level of comfort in our lives. But in reality, that level of comfort is not easily attained throughout one's life. After all, the word "comfort" means different things to different people. For you, comfort could mean having all of your desires met, whereas for others, it could mean having enough food on their plate.

With many of the problems that I have faced in life, there came a time when all I wanted was some comfort, peace of mind, and rest. Finally, I was leaving Egypt with numerous scars, emotional wounds, and mental exhaustion. It was one of the most painful stages in my life. I left my family back in Egypt with a failed business that affected my relationship with my parents, a failed and disastrous marriage then divorce at a very young age, and worst of all, a nearly blind daughter who fell off the balcony as a result of a negligent mother. So, at that stage, I've reached a point in my life where I'd like to be free of all ties to my past.

My brother and I were driving to the airport for my first international flight. Then, while on the bus, I received a phone call. It was a close friend of mine, *Ahamad Sheta*, one of Egypt's most popular songwriters at the time. Our friendship began when I was attempting to become a well-known musician and singer. Knowing that it was him, I handed over my mobile phone to my brother. I requested that he inform Mr. *Sheta* that I had departed the country already.

Having arrived at Cairo Airport, I asked my brother to keep the mobile phone and destroy the sim card within it.

My Wheelchair

Every step I took towards that airplane, I experienced a range of emotions. I was ecstatic, shivering and very nervous. In contrast, I was also feeling some sense of comfort and relief. I was really determined to achieve my goal of focusing on a better future for myself and my family members. The painful memories were heavy baggage that I was willing to abandon forever.

As I stepped onto that massive plane bound for Hong Kong City, I took out a notebook and purposefully wrote a prayer. *"Ya Allah, Almighty God, bestow your blessings and ease on me in this journey,"* I said. *"Allow me to provide for my family through your generosity and assistance, allow me to flourish and succeed, and allow me to taste comfort so that I can provide for my family and daughters. Ameen."*

The prayer was primarily about comfort. I was sick and tired of dealing with problems, particularly financial ones. So going to Hong Kong City was my best chance in life to taste the comfort I was looking for.

When I landed safely in 2001, I was astounded by the beauty of Hong Kong International Airport. The anticipation of starting a new chapter in my life with my new and very kind bride was palpable.

Hong Kong City was, without a doubt, the beginning of true comfort for me. My wife assisted me in finding solid work, and I was able to give a monthly allowance to my family without fail. The days of being broke were no longer

Comfort

part of me. Finally I had my own bank account where I was able to withdraw money from an ATM machine whenever I wanted. For the first time in my life, I felt in charge of my own destiny.

That transformation in my life was exhilarating. I quickly grew accustomed to the comfort and refused to return to the Egyptian way of life. Money, good food, nice clothes, watches, attending events, traveling, and ease on almost every level became suddenly available. As a result, I needed to safeguard that way of life.

Even though I was very happy and became more comfortable than before, the comfort that I experienced in Hong Kong during these days did not make me a good person. In fact, it brought out some real negative traits in me that I was unaware of. I began to lie about the blessings that God Almighty had bestowed upon me; whenever my friends or family members inquired about my situation, I would deny that I was content and living a happy life. Although, which I came to know later, that Allah SWT encourages us to declare and announce His bounties which He provides for us without much fear.

> *"But as for the favor of your Lord, report [it]."*
> Qur'an 93:11

This led to another issue: not assisting people financially when they asked (*other than my family members every month or when they needed*). Although, once again, helping others is a necessity that we need in life, because when we help others, genuinely, Allah SWT intervenes and help us in return. The Prophet Muhammad PBUH once said:

> *"Whoever relieves a believer's distress of the distressful aspects of this world, Allah will rescue him from a difficulty of the difficulties of the Hereafter. Whoever alleviates [the situation of] one in dire straits who cannot repay his debt, Allah will alleviate his lot in both this world and in the Hereafter. Whoever conceals [the faults of] a Muslim, Allah will conceal [his faults] in this life and the Hereafter."* (Muslim)

Simultaneously, I began to get inside my thoughts and feel fantastic about myself. Although I feigned to be in financial difficulty when speaking with my Egyptian pals, connecting with people I knew in Hong Kong was a different story. I started to believe that I was significant and the center of attention in any conversation. To put it another way, I began to become egotistic and pompous.

What struck me the most was the fact that I had forgotten the prayer I had written on the plane before leaving Egypt. I started neglecting my daily prayers and became entirely separated from my religion as a consequence of the excitement that I received in the city, the money that I gained as a result of music production and contractual parties, and of course, the comfort zone that I constructed for myself and refused to step out of.

There's nothing wrong with finding solace, by the way. Comfort, on the other hand, should become a tool for you to grow without disregarding other aspects of your life, particularly your connection with God Almighty.

Here are four things to remember when Allah SWT blesses you and provides you with comfort in this life. Of course, there are more, but these are the ones that speak to me the most. Remember, learn from those who have gone before you and avoid making the same mistakes I did.

1. Share

> *"Those who spend their wealth [in Allah's way] by night and by day, secretly and publicly—they will have their reward with their Lord. And no fear will there be concerning them, nor will they grieve."*
> Qur'an 2:274

When I first arrived in Hong Kong, I used to hide and deny that I was enjoying what God Almighty had bestowed on me. When I was growing up in Egypt, I remember hearing a bizarre "*proverb*" that people would repeat anytime they were gifted with something good: "**hide the blessings or you will lose them.**" "**Watch out, people will be envious of you,**" or they say things like "**protect the candle's flame from the air so that it can light brighter**" to persuade you that you should hide your blessings as much as possible, and that you should also pretend that you're suffering and battling in this world.

My Wheelchair

But when I learned more about Islam, I realized that proclaiming Allah's favor on you is something that is encouraged. It's a time to rejoice and thank Allah, the Almighty, for the blessings you've received. How can you conceal something that you don't even own? The blessings and advantages you receive aren't yours to begin with. In Islam, the topic of *Tawheed* (monotheism) is frequently discussed. This notion encompasses more than just the fact that Allah is the only One who deserves all worship. It also implies that He is the sole ruler, sustainer and maintainer of the universe. If you are a believer, you should have faith in Him, knowing that whatever He orders and whatever He has planned will be carried out exactly as He wishes.

> *"And if Allah should touch you with adversity, there is no remover of it except Him; and if He intends for you good, then there is no repeller of His bounty. He causes it to reach whom He wills of His servants. And He is the Forgiving, the Merciful."*
> Qur'an 10:107

To put it another way, nothing can go beyond Allah's Will, whether good or terrible from our perspective. Because God's Will is always good in all circumstances. So, why are we hiding the blessings He has bestowed upon us? Share it with others and be proud of it.

Take a look at how the language is used here. Allah declares in the first portion of the verse that if Allah should touch you with some adversity, which indicates that adversity has already occurred, then no one except Allah Himself can remove it. But when it came to goodness, He said, "**If He plans for you good**", that means the planned kindness has not yet reached you, but no one can prevent it from reaching you except Him anyway.

So, if we merely accept the truth that goodness and whatever else God has planned for us will pass, shouldn't we remain calm and never deny or hide God's blessings from anyone?

When someone questioned *Al Hasan Al Basry, "What is the secret of your Taqwa/piety?"* he gave, in my opinion, one of the best pieces of advice for keeping us calm when it comes to sharing and publicizing Allah's bounties and blessings upon us. He stated:

- *I understood that my provision and sustenance can never be taken by anyone else other than myself, so my heart is content.*
- *I understood that no one could perform my own actions of worship, so I started to perform them by myself.*
- *I understood that Allah is watching me all the time, so I felt ashamed of doing wrong. And,*
- *I understood that death was waiting for me, so I started to prepare for my meeting with Allah.*

Provision, nourishment, and the benefits that have already been written for you are first on the list, so don't be afraid because no one else will take them but you.

2. Humility

> "...no one humbles himself for the sake of Allah, except that Allah raises him in status."
> Muslim, Kitab Al Birr, Hadith no: 6592 / At Tirmidhi, Kitab Al Birr, Hadith no: 2029

You'd have to come down to earth if you wanted to be at the top. You must ease the air within you and humble yourself before your Creator and His creation if you wish to taste true comfort.

My uncle was bringing our family members back home when he accidentally hit another car and went down to apologize and console the other driver by offering to repair the automobile after ensuring that he was unharmed. The man, on the other hand, was enraged and continued to hurl profanity at my uncle. He even added something along the lines of, *"You have no idea what I'm capable of."* As he returned to his car, the man cried, *"I am (so and so), and this is your very unlucky day."* As he was pulling out his wallet and pointing at his police identity card, baaaaam — a car crashed into him from behind, slamming the door shut and hitting him very hard. We were told he died on the spot.

Remember to be soft and gentle when Allah bestows power, authority, and comfort upon you. Never look down on anyone, and never boast about your position arrogantly, because at the end of the day, we were created from an insignificant drop of liquid, and we will return to the One who created us. In the Qur'an, Allah says:

> *"So let man observe from what he was created. He was created from a fluid, ejected, emerging from between the backbone and the ribs. Indeed, Allah, to return him [to life], is Able. The Day when secrets will be put on trial, then man will have no power or any helper."*
> Qur'an 86:5-10

Reflecting on our origins and where we've come from should humble us as humans. So, no matter how high Allah has raised you, remember that it was He who honors you and brought you to that position. The Qur'an expands on this point:

> *"And it is He who has made you successors upon the earth and has raised some of you above others in degrees [of rank] that He may try you through what He has given you. Indeed, your Lord is swift in penalty; but indeed, He is Forgiving and Merciful."*
> Qur'an 6:165

So, Allah's comfort is a test, a trial, and a means of Allah judging us. And as a result, a reward or punishment will be determined based on how well we perform on that test. So, if you want to get onto the top rank, you'll have to go low, all the way down to the ground, i.e. humility.

The danger of not being humble as a result of comfort, ease, and authority is that you may easily adapt a negative trait

My Wheelchair

that Allah despises and may lead to a harsh fate. That is arrogance, and it is Hellfire.

According to the Prophet Muhammad, PBUH:

> *"He who has in his heart the weight of a mustard seed of arrogance shall not enter paradise."*

What are the possibilities? How many times have our egos caused us to act arrogantly toward one another? As a result, all of us must assess our actions, personalities, and behaviors and make changes as soon as we see that we are headed toward an unwanted and arrogant way of life.

It is said that a man came to the Prophet Muhammad PBUH to embrace Islam, and several of the companions pointed him to the Prophet's location.

The man was apprehensive since he was about to encounter not only the Prophet he had learned about, but also the leader of the Muslims and Arabia at the time, a man of authority and power, and to his surprise, he discovered the Prophet seated on the sand beneath a tree. When The Prophet sensed the man was too scared and nervous, he stood up to greet him, walked over to him, patted his shoulder, and said:

> *"Calm down, I am not a king, I am but the son of a Qurayshi woman who used to eat Qadid (dried meat)."*
> Narrated by Abdullah Ibn-Masoud. From
> "Tahdhibul-Kamal", 141/2

Why, then, did the Prophet quickly recall his modest beginnings? To keep his head down and not let authority or power get into his head so he doesn't react arrogantly to others. This, in my opinion, is the antidote to arrogance. No matter how comfortable you've become in life, you should never forget your poor beginnings. Even if you were born into luxury because your family is wealthy, you should learn to spend time with individuals who are less fortunate than yourself for two reasons: to be grateful for what you have, and to be humbled by sitting with the poor and needy.

3. Nothing is permanent

The death of a dear relative of mine named *Sayed* was the first time in my life that I understood nothing in this world is permanent. In particular, the manner in which he passed away.

For myself and my siblings, Uncle *Sayed* was like a second father. We spent the majority of our childhood in his company. When he arrives home, he usually buys something for us, stays over, and plans fun activities and vacations for us. This man was adored by practically everyone who came into contact with him, not only his family members. The reason for this was his dedication, hard work, and service to everyone he knew or didn't know.

That day is vivid in my memory. My mother was undergoing minor surgery in the hospital, and my sister and I were with her. My father and uncle were at home, preparing to go to the hospital in the afternoon to check on my mother. When my mother had left the operating room, I walked up to phone my father to give him an update on the situation, and while speaking with him, I overheard Uncle *Sayed* say, *"Tell him that I brought him the doughnuts he likes."* After that, I grinned, hung up, and returned to my mother's place.

A few minutes later, I received a phone call from my father through the reception ward where my mother was. *"Please write down this number,"* my father said. That's exactly what I did. *"Call that person and inform him that Uncle Sayed has passed away,"* he continued. *"Wait, what!?"* I yelled. *"When did this happen? How? I just heard his voice!"* At the same time, I was perplexed and enraged.

My father later informed us that following our call, Uncle *Sayed* went to take a nap before heading to the hospital, and when my father went to the room to get something, he discovered that he was gone.

It took me a while to accept that he had died. We were still immature at the time, and we didn't have a lot of faith, but we learnt a valuable lesson. Nothing in this world will last indefinitely. Allah declares:

> *"Everyone upon the earth will perish, And there will remain the Face of your Lord, Owner of Majesty and Honor."*
> Qur'an 55:26-27

Comfort

Knowing that you will depart this planet one day should make you less enthralled with what you have right now. Because when you enter the promised Paradise that Allah has prepared for His virtuous servants, you will find true comfort.

When we experience comfort, we often believe it will endure forever, and we begin to live and die for the material world. Keep in mind that you are only here for a brief time before returning to your Creator to face your Judgment. So, you'd better be ready.

> *"Then did you think that We created you uselessly and that to Us you would not be returned?"*
> Qur'an 23:115

4. Gratitude

> *"... And [remember] when your Lord proclaimed, 'If you are grateful, I will surely increase you [in favor]; but if you deny, indeed, My punishment is severe.'"*
> Qur'an 14:7

In a book titled *Siyara'lam an-Nubula*, Imam *Adh Dhahabi* recounts this story, the narrative of *Abdullah ibn Muhammad*, a righteous individual. During one of his journeys, *Abdullah* became lost in the desert. He came across a tent in the midst of the desert while attempting to locate his way. The tent was ripped in practically every direction. *Abdullah* approached the tent and peered inside out of curiosity. He was surprised to find an elderly gentleman. The man lacked arms and was blind on top of it. While *Abdullah* was trying to make sense of the situation, he noticed that the old man was also paralyzed.

Abdullah was taken aback when he heard the man repeating:

"All Praise is due to Allah who has favoured me over so many of His servants."

"Assalamo Alikum, peace be upon you," *Abdullah* said to the elderly man. "Who is here?" said the elderly gentleman. *Abdullah* explained that he had become disoriented in the desert and ended himself in the tent. *Abdullah* wanted to ask him a question, but the elderly man refused, saying, "I would answer all your questions if you pledge to do me a favor after that." *Abdullah* vowed to do so. Then he asked:

"How could you be in that predicament, with no arms, unable to stand or walk, unable to see at all, and certainly without any riches, yet you are praising Allah for favoring you over others?"

"Have you observed that I am a sensible person?" the old man said thoughtfully. "Yes," *Abdullah* stated emphatically. The man then reasoned with *Abdullah*, asking, "How many of Allah's slaves are insane?" "Probably a lot," *Abdullah* answered. "Then, Alhamdulillah, All Praise is due to Allah who had favoured me over so many of His insane creation," the old man said. He then asked, "Do you not see that I can hear?" *Abdullah* replied, "Yes." After his response, the old man said, "How many of Allah's followers are born deaf, unable to hear?" "Many," *Abdullah* responded. "Then Alhamdulillah, who had chosen me over so many of those who were created deaf," he said.

"Have you noticed that I can talk to you?" the old man asks *Abdullah*. "Indeed, you can," *Abdullah* responded. "How many of Allah's creations are born deafeningly silent and incapable of speaking, as I am?" he inquired once more. "Many," *Abdullah* said. "Then Alhamdulillah, who had chosen me above so many of His mute servants," says the narrator.

The old man then went on to say how fortunate he is to be a Muslim, despite the fact that many people still worship other gods and artifacts aside from Allah.

Then *Abdullah ibn Muhammad* was astounded by the old man's knowledge and faith, and he told him, "Indeed, you uttered the truth. So, what was the favor you were hoping to obtain from me?"

"All of my family members have died," the elderly man explained. I was left with a young boy who goes out every day into the desert to bring me food and assist me with my needs. He went out as normal yesterday, but he hasn't returned until today. So, if you could go out and find him for me, that would be great."

My Wheelchair

Abdullah ibn Muhammad was unfazed. He went out right away to find the youngster. He eventually climbed to the top of a hill, where he discovered some birds circling over what appeared to be prey. *Abdullah* got closer and realized it was the body of a young boy. He was probably attacked by a wolf, who killed him and ate most of his body.

"How will I go back and convey this terribly sad news to the old man who has no one else and nothing at all in this world!" *Abdullah* pondered. *Abdullah* considered not returning to the man several times, but in the end, he decided to return to him.

On the journey back, *Abdullah* thought of Allah's Prophet, Ayub/Job, may peace be upon him. He greeted the elderly man as he entered his tent, and the old man said anxiously, "Did you locate him? Did you find the boy?" as he was certain to see the only person he had ever known.

"Let me ask you this first," *Abdullah* said. "Who is Allah's favorite, you or His Prophet Job?" "No doubt it is Prophet Job," the Old Man responded swiftly. "Whose trial was more difficult, yours or the Prophet Job's?" *Abdullah* said. The old man confirmed that it belonged to the Prophet Job once more. "Seek the recompense and patience from Allah since I have found the small boy on the top of a hill, attacked by a wolf and he has passed away," *Abdullah* told the old man.

The old man immediately said: *"La hawla wa laa quwwata illa billah. Inna lillahi wa inna ilayhi raajioon. Ash shadu alla* ilaha illa Allah." / "There is no power nor might except with Allah. Indeed to Allah we belong and to Him we shall return. I bear witness that none is worthy of worship except Allah."

The old man kept on repeating these words again and again. *Abdullah* noticed that the old man's breath became a bit deep and loud, he gave him water to drink then the old man kept on saying: *"Ash shadu alla ilaha illa Allah, Inna lillahi wa inna ilayhi raajioon / I bear witness that none is worthy of worship except Allah. Indeed to Allah we belong and to Him we shall return,"* until he finally died.

Abdullah ibn Muhammad waited for a while until he came across a group of passing travelers who assisted him in washing the body, shrouding it, and burying it in the desert after praying the funeral prayer for him. *Abdullah* then continued on his journey.

In his dream that night, *Abdullah ibn Muhammad* saw the old man. With his arms and eyesight restored, and his ability to walk, the elderly man appeared to be in great shape.

"How did you end up here and how did you become so well?" *Abdullah* asked the old man in that vision. "My Lord welcomed me into heaven, and it was said to me, *'Peace be upon you for what you have been patient upon, and what a good end you received,"* the old man replied.

This is an incredible narrative from which we can all learn. Whether we are at ease or appear to be in a difficult situation.

My Wheelchair

Remember to thank Allah and praise Him abundantly for all that He has given you. **This is the ultimate comfort.**

Chapter Two

COMFORT-LESS

Comfort-less

Life is not always as stable as we would like. Have you ever been concerned about things going too smoothly? Most of us are afraid that something will go wrong in our lives. We clutch at temporary objects that could vanish in the blink of an eye.

The 5th of April 2020 would be the day that my life would be turned upside down. I had no idea that morning that I would not be able to walk or move on my own in a few hours. My life was about to change for the worst for the rest of my days. I had no idea when I woke up that morning that the incident that was about to happen would send me down a path of despair, fear, and a slew of other emotional battles.

That was the day I had several massive, slipped discs in my lower back.

I'd had a few slipped discs in the past, about fifteen years prior to that day, when I was still living in China and before moving to Australia. The pain was excruciating, and the treatment was lengthy, but in the end, I was able to walk on my own and accept the pain as a necessary part of my life.

But the pain I felt on that day, which had lasted for three or more weeks, was unlike anything I had ever felt in my life. Even thinking about it now makes me feel extremely uncomfortable.

I remember working in my office in our backyard, then going out for some stretching, then using the toilet, and as I was

My Wheelchair

washing my hands between the toilet door and the laundry room, a crashing pain was felt down the lower left side of my back and leg. As a result, I was dragged to the ground and was unable to move an inch. The pain was excruciating, agonizing, and simply unbearable; I was screaming at the top of my voice, and every time I moved, the pain would increase and spread throughout my waist and left leg.

My wife and children rushed to assist, but they were unable to lift me because, once again, every time I moved, the pain would flare up, not only in my lower back and left leg, but now throughout my entire body.

For more than three hours, I was left on the ground in a very uncomfortable position. My painkillers had run out at home, so my wife had to jump in the car and rush to a nearby pharmacy to get me some in the hope of numbing the pain a little. As I waited for any pain reliever, I asked my daughter to get me my cell phone, and then I called a medical service to request a doctor's visit at my house.

I was pinned to the ground around noon as a result of the pain, and doctors weren't available until 5 p.m. What should I do? I didn't have any other choice but to wait.

As my wife returned home with a slew of medications, I took a few tablets and hoped for the best. There wasn't any. All I got was an unpleasant experience, agonizing pain, and despair.

Comfort-less

As the time for the doctor's appointment approached, I remained on the ground, unable to move. I tried one more time, but the pain would flare up throughout my body and snare my nerves. My wife, may Allah bless her, brought a blanket and spread it inch by inch beneath my back, then she and my daughter held the ends of it and dragged me slowly and painfully to my bedroom.

When the doctors arrived, I was told that they could not prescribe injections to relieve the pain faster because they are not authorized to do so during home visits, but they did prescribe some pain relievers and asked me to see my GP the next day.

This happened on Sunday, the day before the start of the new school year, and my school was expecting me the next morning as a student counsellor and teacher. However, the doctors advised me that I might be unable to report to work until I visit my primary care physician. They then gave me a medical certificate and left. And I, too, was left with so many negative thoughts that I struggled with until the following morning.

That evening — I honestly don't want to remember it now that I'm writing about it — was by far one of the worst experiences I've ever had in my life. I was awake all night. My eyes were closed the majority of the time, not because I wanted to sleep or had fallen into a deep slumber, but because I was squeezing all of my facial muscles as a result of the indescribable pain I was experiencing. My body was on high alert and in a state of unrest. I couldn't stay in one place for more than a few seconds. I moved like a snake, left and right, on my sides, sitting, lying down, sitting again, and so on until the early morning hours.

This agony, which I've been seeing in my dreams for the past two weeks, was to be the norm throughout the infamous COVID-19 pandemic era, which coincided with Ramadan 2020. The next morning, after seeing my doctor and getting more medications, CT scans, MRIs, physiotherapy, and so on, I was hit by another slipped disc, this time on the right side.

Despite the fact that the pain was excruciating and difficult to bear, I was still able to stand and walk on my own. However, what happened in the bathroom that day was capable of compressing my nerves beyond even description, adding to my traumatic experience in ways I could never have imagined.

I was putting on my pants after a bath, and as I bent down to put on my left leg, the same painful crash was felt in the lower back of my right leg. That was the final straw. More screams, terrifying pain, numbness in my right leg, and sleepless nights. Until one night, in the middle of the night, I awoke unable to feel my right leg from the knee down. And that was it, I couldn't walk on my own for many months to come.

My wife did everything she could to boost my morale because she saw me becoming sadder and more depressed as a result of the negative thoughts I was resisting. She was encouraging me to walk on my own, holding my hands and looking me in the eyes, lovingly saying, "You can walk." But then she realized I'm too tall and heavier than she is, and I'd be leaning on her with all my weight. Then she made the decision to get me a wheelchair. Despite the fact that she never accepted the idea, she was dealing with the fact that I am unable to walk or stand on my own, at least temporarily.

When I first sat in my wheelchair, I realized I had two choices. To accept my situation, to be sad for a while and get used to it, or to fight until the end, to rely on Allah, and hope for the best. And I opted for the second option. I despised meeting people outside who would stop me and demand a "report" on what had happened to me. I despised seeing their stares fixed on me, as if my wheelchair was a portent of my demise. So, I decided to gather my thoughts, take a deep breath, and write these thoughts down. And so, here are some of the things that kept me hopeful, optimistic, and capable of dealing with this challenge. I termed them the *"Power of the Four As."*

1. **Acknowledge your humanity**

    When the Prophet Muhammad PBUH lost his son, Ibrahim, he wept and cried grimly. When his companions were perplexed as to how he could cry as Allah's messenger, he explained that those tears were mercy from Allah SWT. As a human being

My Wheelchair

like the rest of us, the Prophet PBUH did not fake or hide his emotions when he felt them deep within his heart. He didn't pretend to be strong because, contrary to popular belief, suppressing emotions is not a sign of manhood or strength.

I grew up in a society where crying was frowned upon. "Men don't cry," they'd tell us, so no matter how you felt, as a "real man," you should hide your emotions and pretend that nothing could shake you up.

I've never felt more vulnerable in my life than I did during the first week of my injury. At first, I tried to hold back, to demonstrate to my wife and children that, despite the agonizing pain, I am still strong and capable of enduring anything. It was incorrect; I was superficial, and the pain was multiplied. One was due to the physical disc condition, and the other was due to my attempt to conceal the pain.

But letting it all out made me feel a little better. I didn't care about what society had taught me anymore, so I cried. I didn't care about what was "appropriate," so I screamed at the top of my lungs. I simply let myself express myself truthfully, without regard for what society might think of me; I was simply being me; a man in excruciating pain, and this is how he expresses what he feels.

Comfort-less

I was still young and new to practicing my faith when I performed my Hajj/pilgrimage in 2005. I met an Imam, who also happened to be one of my mentors when I was first learning my religion. As a result, I used to look up to him a lot. Imam *Noorideen Yang*, the organizer of this year's Hong Kong City group, happened to be there.

On the most important day of the Hajj, Arafah — as the Prophet Muhammad PBUH said: *"Hajj IS Arafah."* [Sunan An Nasa'I 3016] — he stood up and began making a Du'a/supplication, which was joined by all members of the group. I relished this moment because I'd been preparing for Arafah for months before we left. But after a few minutes, he ended the Du'a and asked the group to take a nap.

I was dissatisfied, so I approached him and said, "Imam, it's Arafah, how could we rest?"

"Shall we then kill ourselves?" he asked. We were all exhausted, having many elderly pilgrims among us and being on our feet for hours before arriving in Arafah, so naturally we would need a rest. There's no need to exaggerate and pretend you could go on forever. Be yourself, be natural, and take some time to rest.

So, be a human being, cry, feel sad, down, worried, and so on; these are all signs of being a human.

My Wheelchair

And don't ever think that your Iman/faith is weak because you have these moments of annoyance. These moments could mark the beginning of a significant shift in your spiritual journey. Just see what happened as a result of the Ta'ef journey, which was one of the bitterest days in the life of the Prophet Muhammad PBUH. Going through the physical pain as a result of running through rough desert and bleeding all over was necessary for a change to happen. Going through emotional crisis by seeing children stoning him was critical so that victory could taste like nothing else in this world.

On top of that, if you pass these moments, which are tests from Allah SWT, you will be richly rewarded. Because you accepted the Qadar/destiny written by Allah SWT for you.

2. **Accept reality**

During these days, there was nothing I could do. I had done everything I could to stand on my own, but every time I tried, I fell either on the ground or back into my bed.

After one of the conferences in Malaysia, I received a phone call in my hotel room. A young boy approached me and requested to speak with me; the volunteers kindly gave him my room number. As soon as I responded, he began telling me about his father, who died recently, and how he still can't believe he died. He said that his father was young, that he was nice to everyone, that he was religious, and so on, all of which are not reasons to be immune from death. As a result, I realized that the individual requires assistance on a different level, possibly psychologically.

Refusing to accept reality may have the opposite effect. A life of delusion that will prevent you from progressing and achieving your goals. Consider the following questions:

a) Am I responsible for what happened?

> If the answer is YES, keep in mind that we are all human and make mistakes. So, instead of getting stuck, get back on your feet and get things done, no matter how difficult the journey is. And if the answer is NO, then don't torture yourself through the endless blame game.

b) Can you change the situation you are in?

> If the answer is YES, then go ahead and do it. Regardless of how long it takes you. Don't focus on the end result right now; instead, focus on reversing the situation in your favor with all available resources. However, if the

answer is NO, then accept it. Leave it out and consider how to move forward in life in a different way.

In other words, change what you can control and leave out what you can't.

3. **Arrange your thoughts**

When I was diagnosed with this illness, I was going insane, battling a lot of negative thoughts. However, I realized that I was no longer assisting myself, and the people around me began to avoid me as a result of this dark period in my life. I became extremely toxic to others, including my family. Then I did a few things to help myself and those around me.

a) I slowed down

I gave myself a space to recover. I was familiar with neurology and how our nervous system functions. I was aware that my condition had a high level of nerve compression, which could result in nerve damage or pressure that requires specific exercise or, in my case, surgery to begin the healing process. So, I knew I'd need more time to heal, and my mind began to slow down.

b) Journaling

Writing down my thoughts and insights from books I was reading from my bedside, the Qur'an, and other sources, helped me a lot with clarity and hope. I was able to express my emotions to a nonjudgmental friend, my journal. I was able to say everything I needed to say without expecting people to object or to explain what they thought was right or wrong. I was simply liberated and secured.

c) Listening to motivational lectures and talks

What have other people done to deal with their difficulties? What is the meaning of these trials and tribulations? The more I listened to other people's traumatic stories the less I thought about my own problems. That is why I recognized the wisdom of the Prophet Muhammad's narration when he said, *"Look at those beneath you and not at those above you, for it is more appropriate that you should not consider Allah's blessing as less." Sunan Ibn Majah 4142*

4. Appreciate

My Uncle Ibrahim, one of my favorite uncles, died after a long battle with cancer. I asked him one day when I met him, I believe a few months before his death, "Are you all right? Be patient, uncle." He unexpectedly smiled and said, **"Why shouldn't I be fine? Allah had blessed me with 60 years of complete enjoyment, comfort, and ease before testing me for a few years with pain, sickness, and discomfort. Shouldn't I be thankful for the first 60 years and wait for the rest?"** I was astounded by this man's level of patience. He not only accepted what Allah had tested him with, but he also remembered to be grateful for all of the good days he had throughout his life.

Also, keep in mind Allah SWT expiates your past sins, which you have most likely forgotten, with every painful moment you experience in this world. *"Never a believer is afflicted with discomfort, illness, anxiety, grief, or mental worry, or even the pricking of a thorn,"* said the Prophet Muhammad PBUH, *"but Allah will expiate his sins on account of his patience."* Riyad as-Salihin 37

So always be reminded with the **4 As** formula when you are struck with challenges and trials in life. Acknowledge your humanity, accept your reality, give yourself time to arrange your thoughts, and appreciate what you already have been blessed with.

Chapter Three

EMOTIONAL BATTLES

When life throws you a curveball, you'll experience a variety of fears. The question is, how will you deal with these terrifying monsters? Trials and tribulations are inevitable in our mortal lives. Will you allow your anxieties to take control of your life and have a bad impact on you or face whatever may come along and stand your ground?

Allah SWT said in the Qur'an:

> *"Do the people think that they will be left to say, 'We believe' and they will not be tried? But We have certainly tried those before them, and Allah will surely make evident those who are truthful, and He will surely make evident the liars."*
> Qur'an 29:2-3

It was a difficult night. I was struggling to use the bathroom and didn't want to wake up my wife, who had already been exhausted by my illness. I attempted to drag my heavy legs to the ground in the hope of walking, however slowly, to the toilet. But as expected, I was thrown to the ground, and my wife awoke terrified and rushed to help me get back on my feet.

"How come you didn't wake me up?" she yelled. "I didn't want to disturb you," I said quietly.

My wife then yanked me up with all her might until I could sit back down on the bed. She then assisted me in getting to the toilet and back to bed, which was excruciatingly painful.

My Wheelchair

She then covered me, checked to see if I was okay, then went back to the other side of the bed and promptly fell asleep.

But what about my situation? Nowadays, it is rare to get a full night's sleep. It was only a wish, one I was certain would never come true. Hope is nothing more than a delusion and a lie that keep you waiting for nothing but pain and difficulties. My hoping was changing my entire being into the worst version of myself. A toxic hope that trapped and imprisoned me on multiple levels. Not just physically, but emotionally as well.

That night, I began my battles with my emotions. I began the race with my intense negative thoughts that had suddenly taken over my entire being. That night, I believed or convinced myself that hope had been lost and could never be found or returned one day. It was that dark night when I realized, without hesitation or doubt that nothing could ever get me back on my feet. I hoped too much; every day when I opened my eyes, I would try to move my toes to see if the numbness had subsided or my legs had completely stopped. It was a constant nightmare of hope.

I hoped to get out of bed quickly, as I used to, and wake my kids up for prayers. I hoped to turn on my side of the bed and fall asleep quickly. On weekends, I hoped to take my family to soccer matches. I hoped to take them to their favorite restaurants. I had hoped to play soccer with my son in the backyard and teach him some essential skills. I hoped to scare and tease my daughter by unexpectedly entering her room and having fun with her. I hoped and hoped, but all I got was emotional torture, which was just as painful as the physical one.

That night, I told myself, "I admit it. I can't fight any longer. I can't wait for something that I'm certain will never return." I was completely convinced. "The fight is over." I comforted my defeated self.

And you might be wondering right now, "Where is his faith!?" Isn't he the *Sheikh* who has been lecturing us on patience? Isn't he supposed to be more powerful than the rest of us? Where are the Qur'anic verses now? Where are his reminders to expect Allah's rewards?

Isn't this a strange situation?

Let me remind you all of one thing. Humanity. In Chapter Two we discussed humanity and how acknowledging that very visible aspect of our lives brought peace and contentment to my soul when I was distressed at the start of my injury. Don't ever think that life for public figures is easy and perfect. We, too, have our flaws and, on occasions, our low points. Accepting that part of our lives and being completely natural about it is what will restore our peace and contentment.

During these trying evenings, I went through a series of emotional conflicts and worries that provided me with a wealth of new insights, comfort, and strengths. Despite that terrifying sensation known as fear, I was able to emerge from this phase with a wealth of learning and benefits after convincing myself, with great conviction, that I am a loser and of no use.

Fear of losing something

It's not as simple as having what you appreciate on hand and then losing it the next second. It's not easy to take for granted that you can spring out of bed every morning, only to be paralyzed, powerless, and unable to control even your smallest toe in a matter of minutes. Every night, as I hoped for a better scenario, I heard voices in my head telling me, "Forget it. It's finished." I was terrified of losing my ability to walk and move as freely as I did before. This is the definition of anxiousness, which I had no idea at the time that one day I may experience it. Even though I'd seen it in other people's lives, I never imagined I'd be the one to suffer its merciless treatment.

Fear of losing my mobility and being confined to a wheelchair for the rest of my life, racing thoughts, quick heartbeats, shivering — it's dreadfully painful, exhausting, and stressful. When you let your thoughts run wild, they take over every aspect of your being.

But then it occurred to me.

Emotional Battles

"Inna LillahiWa Inna IlayhiRaj'ioon! / Indeed we belong to Allah, and indeed to Him we will return."
Qur'an 2:156

My entire self does not belong to me. Not to mention my legs or any other portion of my body. A Qur'anic passage that I used to recite over and over again. A verse that we are recommended to recite anytime we hear something negative or lose someone we love. Yes, I have lost certain physical abilities, but I am still sane, can operate properly, and continue the wonderful work that my family and I have begun.

Okay, okay... "Slow down," I told myself. I then pondered: "How do I deal with losing something I once had? What is the best way to deal with these feelings?"

The solution was found in another story.

I was with Mohamed Atallah, my best friend, at his house one day when I smelled a very nice fragrance. If you don't already know, one of the things that makes me happy is fine perfume. So, I immediately inquired about the brand, where he got it, and so on, and the story was over, or so I thought.

But just as I was about to leave, I greeted my friend, and as usual, we shook hands and hugged tightly, before he gently dropped the bottle of perfume into my pocket. And, of course, I pretended that he shouldn't have done it and that there was no need for his generous gesture, but on the inside, I was overjoyed.

The ultimate solution to overcoming the fear of losing something is to become a giver. Not to cling to possessions as if you'll be granted immortality and be able to enjoy them indefinitely. The ultimate and most comfortable solution to our misery of the fear of losing something is to learn to let go of what we cling to in this world.

God Almighty said in the Qur'an:

> *"Never will you attain the good [reward] until you spend [in the way of Allah] from that which you love. And whatever you spend — indeed, Allah is Knowing of it."*
> Qur'an 3:92

Despite the fact that the verse is about spending your material possessions, I found it to be very relevant to my experience. By writing this book, I decided to give back that experience and share what happened to me and how I was able to cope with my difficult days. So remember this if you're afraid of losing anything.

Fear of pain

Is it possible to see your agony in your dreams?

Yup. That was something I did. Pain appeared to me in dreams as an ugly, scary, and very disturbing figure that would snare my nerves and cause me to scream and call for help, despite the fact that I don't recall sleeping for the first two to three weeks after that incident when I was knocked out by the extreme and unbearable ache.

I used to take my medication at night to numb my body and enjoy what is known as a 'high' by those who use drugs — this feeling of total relaxation and euphoria would at least get me some comfort before another nerve pinch caused me to jump out of bed screaming.

How to face your pain

We were taught as children that bad emotions should be avoided. But happiness and optimism aren't the only emotions that should be permitted to exist. We are human beings who experience a variety of emotions throughout our lives. Accepting what appear to be negative feelings rather than avoiding them is part of having a healthy view.

When faced with a crisis, we should be courageous and not force ourselves to hide our feelings, especially if we are harmed. Remove the belief that expressing emotions will bother others. Humans, on the other hand, are wired to avoid suffering. Attempting to suppress the discomfort will cause more harm than good.

However, whether or not we choose to face it is entirely up to us as individuals. After all, facing adversity is the foundation of strength and opportunity. Who knows what kind of growth awaits us on the other side.

Fear of the night

The night is a typical occurrence in our life on this planet. For some, it is the most peaceful time of their day, but for others, nightmares will resurface. I used to despise the darkness of the evening when I was a kid. Saying goodnight meant I was going to give in to my worries. My father would patch any hole and keep the light from entering before sleeping, so I had trouble breathing and going to sleep every night when I was young. In my head, I imagined myself dying because I couldn't breathe.

Going to school was difficult too because I hadn't gotten enough sleep. I remembered that I would be awake for several hours, waiting for the ray of sunshine to rise so that I may fall asleep. I kept my fears to myself and kept them hidden from others.

Meanwhile, the night was supposed to be mine to enjoy. I used to spend my adolescent years doing things like singing in nightclubs and attending weddings. Arriving home early in the morning, while others were getting ready for the day.

To be honest, it took me a long time to overcome my fear of darkness, and it wasn't until I got married that I was able to do so. By becoming who I am today, I believe I was able to overcome my fears. I was no longer afraid of dying because God decides our time anyway. I gave up my life to him, and whatever happens to me will be accepted openly — so why the fear? Yes, death is a scary topic to discuss, but interestingly, the Prophet Muhammad PBUH advised us to speak about it often. Why? Because it is the inevitable reality.

When I was injured, I had similar nightmares at night when I had these slipped discs. The fear of experiencing the same pain or seeing these ghostly figures in my dreams. The fear of seeing my pain as a result of medication. Fortunately, *Ramadan*, the fasting month, has a plethora of resources. I would spend the night watching lectures and listening to powerful reminders to ease these moments of fear.

How to face the fear of the dark and have restful sleep

If, like me, you used to be afraid of the dark, this will allow you to function normally again. First, you should understand why you are afraid of the dark. Addressing your fears rather than hiding them from others will greatly benefit you. Second, alter your sleeping environment to one that relaxes your body and soothes your mind.

Professional assistance is an option, particularly if the problem is interfering with your daily life. Finally, self-help tools like books can help you re-examine your internal thoughts and anxieties. And before any of the above, calling upon Allah SWT when you experience those fearful moments is essential. Here are some of what the Prophet PBUH taught us to recite in these situations:

My Wheelchair

"Oh Allah, I seek refuge in you from the difficulties of hardships. And the acquisition of wretchedness, and ill-fate, and the enemy's malicious rejoicing for my suffering."

Next, Abdullah ibn Mas'ood RA narrates that whenever Prophet Mohammad PBUH used to be afflicted with any concern or stressful situations he would recite this supplication:

At-Tirmidhi

"O Allah, I seek refuge with You from anxiety, and sorrow, and weakness, and laziness, and miserliness, and cowardice, and the burden of debts and from being overpowered by men."
Bukhari No# 2893, 5425, 6363, 6369; Abu Dawud No# 1541; At-Tirmidhi No# 3484; An-Nasa'i No# 5449, 5450, 5453, 5476

Sleep is essential for survival, which is why I value it so highly in my life. Sleep is sometimes sacrificed in order to achieve other goals or fulfill obligations. However, it has an impact on our bodies and how we function in our daily lives. Don't be like me when I was younger and couldn't focus in class because I wasn't getting enough sleep.

After all, it is an opportunity for our brains to cleanse themselves. There would be many pages of information to write if I were to list down all the benefits of sleeping in my book. Getting enough sleep helps your immune system to function properly, resulting in a healthy body. Furthermore, it alleviates stress, which leads to a positive mood and attitudes. Remember, having enough sleep does not in any way mean to sleep too much, rather, to understand when to sleep, how many hours are needed and so on and to do that to the best of your ability.

Fear of the unknown

We require jobs in order to achieve the stability and security that we seek. This is a reality that we cannot avoid. In Hong Kong, I was accustomed to a certain level of comfort, but life is unpredictable. As I received an offer to work in Australia, my wife decided to close her business in China and I passed on to a dear friend of mine, all of the rights of the organization that I once owned in Hong Kong. But then, my fear of the unknown struck when I started reflecting over what could happen later on to me and my family if things didn't work out the way we envisioned it. Worse, what would happen now with me being pinned to my wheelchair and unable to work like before? Will the school managers ask me to leave? Where will I go to if that happened?

Returning to Hong Kong was impossible since I did not have permanent residency there, and I did not intend to go back to Egypt. My family would have a difficult time assimilating to the lifestyle and culture of Egypt if I were to decide to live there with them.

My Wheelchair

Because my wife and children lived in mainland China, we used to meet every two to three weeks in Hong Kong City. Australia, on the other hand, gave us the stability that we were craving.

My ideal career would be that of a school counselor where I work currently, and my major would be Islamic studies and religious teacher. My condition after the injury was well-understood by the school management and I'm also so grateful to the Australian government for allowing persons with disabilities to work, function and excel within the society. Hence, I was not fired as a result of my physical restrictions and limitation. Thank God.

Just seeing my school management supporting me in all directions, changed my perspective on being fearful of the unknown. I started to let Allah SWT be in control of my provision and as a result, my worries vanished. I am not afraid of the unknown anymore since it is God Almighty alone who provides to those who seek and work hard.

"If you are grateful, I will surely increase you [in favor];"
Qur'an 14:7

The majority of us are always on the lookout for our neighbors' greener side. We focus on what we don't have and whine about how unjust the world is. Happiness is difficult to achieve if each of us focuses on what we lack. Complaining will only result in a waste of time and resentment.

Always remember to count your blessings rather than your troubles, no matter what you're going through. After all, problems are an inevitable part of our existence on this planet; if we don't have them, then we would be living in paradise. But since we aren't there yet, we should cultivate appreciation in the midst of our struggles.

Through prayer, we develop gratitude to Allah SWT for showering us with His bounties. The Prophet Muhammad PBUH used to pray for an hour or two every night until his feet swelled and bled. His wife questioned his behavior, but he responded that despite his suffering, he should be thankful and grateful to Allah SWT. Despite my life's challenges and tribulations, I'm grateful. If you count your blessings, you will be overwhelmed by their magnitude and the outcome that Allah SWT will surprise you with.

Fear of Allah's anger

Things aren't going well in your life, and you're wondering if it's because of something you've done in the past and it's haunting you now . . . Yes my friend, I've been there too. As humans, we want to know why we are experiencing these tragedies and afflictions. At one point, I was afraid that what had occurred to me was due to Allah's wrath. My injuries, I believed, were a result of my life's sins.

I was never the type of person who always cared about religion when I was younger. I was a mischievous and

My Wheelchair

disobedient son to my parents from an early age, causing them a great deal of grief. Furthermore, as I indicated in Chapter One, I've had disastrous relationships, including one with my previous wife, which ended in divorce.

I never imagined I'd be able to walk again at the time. I couldn't tell whether it was a reward or a punishment. And because of the depressive state that I was in, I was more inclined to God's punishment than His rewards.

But then I remembered, that if this is my expectation of God, then this is what I will receive from Him on the Day of Judgment.

> *"Allah the Almighty said: **I am as My servant thinks I am. I am with him when he makes mention of Me. If he makes mention of Me to himself, I make mention of him to Myself; and if he makes mention of Me in an assembly, I make mention of him in an assembly better than it. And if he draws near to Me an arm's length, I draw near to him a cubit, and if he draws near to Me a cubit, I draw near to him a fathom. And if he comes to Me walking, I go to him at speed.***"
> It was related by al-Buhkari (also by Muslim, at-Tirmidhi and Ibn-Majah).

Thus, I decided to go to Allah SWT crawling. No matter what is happening, I will not let myself to despair and lose such company. The fear of Allah means to realize that your disobedience will ultimately lead to destruction and punishment. Fear of Allah also means to do what He has commanded and to avoid all His prohibitions. And if you lived with these principles, then your pain is a reward from Allah to elevate your status and not a punishment. God willing.

Chapter Four

THE WAIT

The Wait

Nobody wants to go through physical or emotional pain. We would rather do anything than suffer through the agony of pain. But pain, whether emotional, physical, mental, or otherwise, is part of our existence. Hence, we need to deal with it rather than avoid it.

> *"We have certainly created man into hardship."*
> Qur'an 90:4

This is the time when we pause to reflect on our lives. We may be so preoccupied with our daily obligations that we rush through it. However, a single event has the potential to alter our perspective of life and bring down the entire world crashing over our heads.

The first two nights after my injury were like a lifetime of nightmares. I couldn't sleep because the pain was constantly coursing through my body. When my wife was sleeping, I could hear the clock ticking as if it was a hammer smashing my head. My lower body was constantly sending pain up and down my spine. I couldn't find any comfortable position to rest my body. I was leaning with my right side against the wall next to my bed hoping to steal a slumber, but was never able to.

My wife, may Allah bless her and reward her abundantly, would pile up pillows around me to make me feel better but the comfort would last only for a few seconds. It was less painful when my legs were on the ground, but when I put them on the bed, it was excruciating. I hadn't gotten any sleep in two days or even more. It was horrible seeing

My Wheelchair

images in my mind as a result of the medications and being drained from the pain. I just wanted the pain to stop, but that wish was never granted.

These were the moments that I started to reflect and recall the pain-free life that I had prior to this incident. We usually fantasize about how we used to be free of all these ills only when we are struck with illness. We're left wondering why we're in this situation and how to reverse it in our favor. What did we do wrong? Is this our punishment or merely a test of faith?

After suffering from those sleepless nights, I was able, by Allah's aid, to pass these moments of literal torture as a result of the following:

1. **Get busy**

    It is because of this chance and severe test that we have so many hours to fill in our days. Especially at times like this, when we want to divert our attention away from the pain we are feeling. There are many ways to cope with pain, some of which are good and some of which are really not so.

    While I was injured, I wrote this book. Because the pain could not be alleviated, I devised alternative ways to spend my time. Despite my condition, I tried to be productive. This is a collection of all of my thoughts, ideas, and notes from that time period. A BOOK.

It occurred to me at the time that my recorded journey could help me and other people who are living and are experiencing a similar fate. So, I started to listen to lectures and motivational speeches every morning. At the same time, I would scribble notes in my diary and relate what I've learned from my current situation. I also started to interact with my family members and enjoy their company instead of taking my frustration out on them.

Doing all of these things kept me from obsessing over my condition and pain. These activities, such as listening to other resources, writing, and engaging with my family in decent discussions have altered my way of thinking. It has provided me with a viewpoint that would greatly benefit me in my journey of recovery.

With the internet at our fingertips, there is no excuse not to learn something new or to seek out some inspiration. The bottom line is, get yourself busy with something that you love and the pain will subside.

2. **Use your free time**

Consider the activities that you enjoy. It can be anything as long as it benefits you and improves your overall well-being. Time, unlike other resources on Earth, cannot be replenished. You have complete control over how your time is divided and spent, so make the most of it.

The Prophet Muhammad PBUH said, "There are two blessings in which many people incur loss. (They are) health and free time (for doing good)."
Al Bukhari - Riyad as-Salihin 97

3. Don't be afraid to try new things

Are you the type of person who never considers himself to be a reader? Or perhaps there are activities that you consider to be out of character for you. Don't be afraid to try new things and activities that can change your life and provide you with some hormonal rush that will assist you along the journey of recovery. And of course, it goes without saying that these activities should be done according to what pleases Allah SWT. If, for example, you consider yourself a terrible writer, don't let this limiting belief stop you from trying out this amazing skill.

4. Record your journey

You should document this period of your life in whatever way you can. I, for example, am grateful that I was able to collect and document these experiences. This allows you to return to that point in time and reflect on what you went through, how you behaved, what could've been done better and how to improve if things went down the same path again. This will give you an idea of your personal strengths and weaknesses. And the next time adversity comes your way, you'll know you'll be able to face it head on, just like the others.

5. **The power of Du'a and prayers**

I was a singer and musician once as many of you are aware, and that was a big part of my life. When Leslie Cheung committed suicide, it prompted me to rekindle my relationship with God Almighty. When I was in Hong Kong, he was my role model, and I aspired to be just like him in every way. I aspired to achieve his success on every level, believing that this would be the final ingredient in my happiness.

When he died in this manner, I realized that I might end up just like him. I was wondering, if he had it all, why wasn't he happy and content? I remember him leaving a suicide note that said *"depression."* Why was *depression* the only fate for someone who has accumulated *all* of what we think are reasons for us to be happy? This was a massive wake-up call for me.

I couldn't sleep at the time because I was afraid I would die in my bed. I used to go to Church every

My Wheelchair

Sunday with my wife who was a Catholic Christian at that time, but then I quickly decided not to go again. Then one night I woke up and said, "*I want to pray.*" I grabbed my prayer mat, started reciting the Qur'an calmly, bowed before Allah SWT and prostrated then I started to feel more at ease. The process of practicing Islam did not happen overnight, but prayer was the take-off that made everything else smooth and easy.

My wife became interested in Islam over time as a result of the same prayers. It took her a while to decide, but finally she was able to make a conscious decision about embracing and practicing Islam. Since that day, we both started the journey of learning more about Islam and putting knowledge into practice as much as we can.

Prayers, especially the five obligatory ones are very essential in our lives. Salah or prayer IS the most important of all pillars and the foundation of our religion. Despite the fact that I was in a wheelchair, I made an effort to beg Allah SWT every day and every night to help me with this difficult challenge. I kept asking Allah SWT either He should take away the pain or make it a reason for me to reap its benefits in the afterlife.

Du'a/supplication, on the other hand is the heartfelt dialogue we have with our Creator. It is not only for ourselves, but also for those who have played an important role in our lives. We can lose sight of the fleeting nature of this world at times. As a result, we should be reminded that there is an afterlife that exists beyond what we are experiencing right now. Clinging to our possessions and connections in this material world is what brings most sadness and grief to our lives.

We should offer our sincere prayers to Allah SWT and remember to keep this conversation no matter what we're going through in life. At the end of the day, it is just a life that one day will come to an end. We need to ask ourselves, are the anxieties that we're experiencing just because we are afraid to lose our worldly status? We know that chasing wealth and fame will only leave us empty and depressed. That's why the connection with God should always be maintained and practiced. Why? Because:

"... the Hereafter is better and more enduring."
Qur'an 87:17

6. **Battling instant gratifications**

I'm not the perfect man who never makes a mistake. I, like everyone else, am susceptible to life's temptations. But I can't use this as an excuse to avoid doing what will improve my life.

My Wheelchair

I used to be a very impatient young boy. I needed things right now and would cry if I didn't get them. I remember a long time ago, during *Ramadan*, we had a regular meal of baked beans that I loved so much and it was our tradition at home to have this meal every night during breaking our fast. But one day, my mother forgot to buy them, which disappointed me to the core and as a result, I decided NOT to eat that night. Despite the fact that everyone was pleading with me to let this go that day, I insisted on making that horrible scene until very late that night. I literally made everyone at home angry and disgusted with my behavior for the sake of pleasuring my stomach.

Looking back at this incident now, I know it should never be repeated in my present day.

Just like fast food. The convenience of having ready-made food and the irresistible taste of oil and salt are absolutely enjoyable, but the benefit you are receiving is nearly nil. Yes, sometimes eating at these restaurants would save a lot of time, but that positive side of saving time is harmful to our health in the long term.

Music was a part of my past which made my life entertaining, exciting and busy. But all these came at a cost. The entertainment industry offers many temptations that can sway people off the true path of Allah SWT. So I decided to quit it. Even though I loved music so much I quit because it would lead me to inappropriate behaviors and sinful activities.

In the early '90s, pornographic material streamed through society via VHS tapes and magazines. These disturbing images offer young people an escape from the reality of life, leading them to temporary pleasure and enjoyment. This escapism, most of the time, turns into pornographic addiction that damages the lives of its consumers for many years to come. That's why Allah SWT commanded us to hold our sexual desires until we are capable of getting married.

"And they who guard their private parts, except from their wives or those their right hands possess, for indeed, they will not be blamed — But whoever seeks beyond that, then those are the transgressors."
Qur'an 23:5-7-

That's why, one of the solutions being discussed on various levels and settings today is delayed gratifications.

My Wheelchair

What are the benefits of delayed gratification?

Is it possible to have fun in life? Of course, it is good to pursue life's pleasures. However, there are consequences and trade-offs with every decision we make. We are humans, and we must consider the long-term consequences of our actions.

Delaying gratification is a difficult task, especially when your surroundings encourage you to enjoy the present moment and forget about your worries. But in reality, life isn't all about having fun and being happy. There is more to life than just enjoying our pleasures at will.

We should be patient in waiting for the results and not expect our efforts to be rewarded immediately. Having this mindset will benefit us in a variety of ways. For starters, it forces us to consider the consequences of our actions. Second, we would have an effect on others as well as ourselves. After all, we do not exist as solitary individuals, and our actions do have an impact on others.

Waiting for a relief

When we face adversity, we wait.

I was sure that Allah SWT was testing me and my faith. So, I was hoping that one day I'll be able to walk again and enjoy the limbs that He created for me. I increased my prayers and worship for Him. I was certain that God

The Wait

Almighty would provide me with what I desired. But at the same time, I also knew, that what I desire is not necessarily good for me. So I waited for Him to decide the best for me.

I am aware that our brains can change and adapt, so I started to shift my mindset from being pessimistic to optimistic, that Insh a Allah, one day my condition would improve. That long wait may be unpleasant for others, but I choose to make it enjoyable for myself. **Waiting for Allah's relief is an act of worship** because you made Him the focus of your life in sorting out your misery, sadness, and grief.

If you are experiencing a slow period and don't know what to do, just be patient and think positively. Put your trust and faith in Allah SWT that He is capable of either changing the situation NOW or rewarding you for your patience later. So let Allah SWT assist you on His terms and have faith that he will grant your wishes.

Chapter Five

PAIN TO GAIN

As I indicated in previous chapters, in life it is not always a happy ride. There are sufferings and struggles that will arrive. The question is, will this make you stronger or weaker as a person?

It was when a photo of mine circulated the internet that people became curious about my condition. I've admitted that at first, I didn't want to be seen as a victim of life. I didn't want to be pitied and asked repeatedly about my injury. In fact, the most painful moment, at that time, was to be asked, "Why did you end up like this?"

From a person that used to encourage others and infuse faith and hope into their lives, I'd become the bitterness of my fate. Things started to make no sense at all.

Thinking that no one has a right to advise me because they are not experiencing what I'm going through, I started, unreasonably, hating these situations. From the joyful person that I was, I was transformed into a resentful one.

Then a realization hit me. What if there are people experiencing the same pain as me? Or even worse! So, I've decided to speak about my pain instead of waiting for others to ask about it. I went online, I posted videos, and wrote blogs with the intention of inspiring others who are going through any type of pain. And interestingly, this helped me to find a new mission in life, which is inspiring the Muslim community and hopefully helping them cope with their pain and challenges in life.

You see this simple action made me remove the focus on my own pain outside of myself. I stopped telling myself to be a victim of my circumstances. That shift of my mindset was capable of relieving my tensions. It was the stepping stone to where I'm at today. On my feet.

Here are the lessons that I would teach based on the pain that I've experienced in those difficult days. I hope this will shed some light, for others that feel hopeless in their situation.

Positive life stance

Is wallowing in negativity going to change anything? This is a question for those that are blinded by their problems. Sometimes there are things that are totally out of our control. Instead, put your energy on things that you can control or change.

When I was in that position, I decided to focus on thinking about what I can do and not what I can't. From this experience I always remind myself, family members, and my students to focus on the solution and not on the problem.

1. **Identify the negative thoughts that are running through your mind**

    It is essential that we be completely honest with ourselves. No more pretending that we are okay especially if we know deep inside that this is not the case. If possible, you could journal these thoughts so that you can look back at them and identify what made you feel the way you feel and what can be done to change your situation for the better.

2. **Think of ways to be productive**

    You know within yourself that there are activities that you could do instead of drowning in negative thoughts and pessimism. If you have no idea then it is perfectly okay to explore areas that are outside of your comfort zone. This may be writing like I did, reading books, watching documentaries and many more.

3. **What if what you're doing is considered by others as unproductive?**

    The truth is we all have different versions of what we consider as productive. This is not the time to judge yourself and worry if your activity meets the standards of other people. Focus on your life and what you think your authentic self would be happy to do.

    It's okay to start with a plan, envisioning yourself with a hopeful outlook on life. Dream of what you can do with your current state and trust yourself that you could accomplish your plan. For example, I imagined myself being productive while I was in

My Wheelchair

my wheelchair. In short, thinking of the ways you could DO things instead of crying over what you're unable to do due to your pain and limitation.

Pain and creativity

Even when I was experiencing pain, I was writing this book. This was more than being productive at that time. It gave me the boost that I needed. In addition, I knew that my writing could help others who are going through similar scenarios. I admit that at one point the pain was capable of breaking me and my spirit of writing and creating. It let me experience the despair of not continuing my goals and dreams in life. But I'm so thankful that I did not succumb to the darkness of these painful moments and quit my journey. It's like I found my purpose even though I was not in the best or most comfortable position in my life.

1. **Create something**

   It is not just the special few that can create wonderful things. Think of yourself as a unique individual that has a different story to tell. No matter what form of creativity that you choose to produce, it is worthwhile to try. Grab anything and let your creativity flow. Don't compare your work with others. Instead of competing, learn and be inspired by the beauty and diversity in Allah's creation.

2. **Express your thoughts and feelings**

   If you're from a society that discourages expressing certain types of emotions then it would be a refreshing start to change this belief. Accept your emotions as part of being who you are as a human being. Always remember that having them will not make you weak. **Emotions were created to be felt**. Not only that, no matter how intense they are, we, as human beings, **were created with the ability to handle them**. Allah SWT stated:

   > *"Allah does not charge a soul except [with that within] its capacity."*
   > Qur'an 2:286

   After all, if you are avoiding and battling them, then you may end up developing horrible habits like drinking alcohol, pornography, taking drugs and many more. So, let them out, reasonably and wisely, and express them with someone you trust.

3. **Avoid perfectionism**

   Honestly, I used to struggle with perfectionism in my work and almost every other area of my life. I used to sacrifice family time to feel that what I would put out there is my best work. Looking back, I regret the wasted time. Yes, that was a wasted time that I could've spent to cherish the moments with my loved ones instead.

Worse, I used to always delay decisions with the excuse of waiting for the 'perfect time.' So let me remind you of one thing. The perfect time, at all times, is NOW.

So, instead of waiting for the perfect moment, I decided to share my work and my story. Even if I viewed it as half-baked, it is more important that it is out and has finally seen the light. All that I can do now is to observe the feedback and make the necessary changes continuously.

Things that needed to change

As I'm at a new chapter in my life, I will describe the errors that I've made in the past which resulted in a lot of negativities when coping with my injury. Why is this important? Because the past actions that we did contribute to our present and future states. I've made mistakes that I've regretted until today and may Allah SWT forgive us all. Ameen

1. **Admit your mistakes**

    Look at your past actions and list all the errors that you've committed. This is not to blame or torture yourself but to learn from the errors that you've made and avoid them in the future. Prevent yourself from putting the responsibility on other people especially if you're the one who committed these errors. It is indeed easier to pin the blame to things that are outside of ourselves. But how can we learn with this mindset?

Also, what can help you achieve this point is repenting to Allah SWT. Because one of the conditions of repentance is to admit your wrongs.

2. **Apologize and humble yourself**

No matter the reason for your bad actions, don't justify them. Set aside your ego and humble yourself to the point that you could say you're sorry. There's no use of being proud and waiting for the other side to apologize first. You don't want your heart to be filled with hatred and bitterness before departing this world. Apologizing means that you've admitted your imperfections and given yourself a chance to be forgiven. It is also one of the gates that may elevate you to the highest levels of Paradise.

The Prophet Muhammad PBUH said:

"Whoever humbles himself by a degree for Allah, glory be to Him, Allah will raise him by a degree. Whoever is arrogant to Allah by a degree, Allah will lower him by a degree until he is made 'the lowest of the low.'"
Source: Sunan Ibn Mājah 4176

3. **Reflection**

It is not just the words that should be promised but the change in behavior. We need to let ourselves reflect on how we arrived at our mistakes. This is to prevent the errors from repeating themselves or preventing us from creating a habitual and addictive cycle of sins. Set aside "alone time" with your thoughts, notepad, and a pen. Look at the past with open eyes, then design the future while asking Allah SWT for assistance.

Reconnection with family

One of my biggest regrets in the past was not spending enough quality time with my family members. Indeed, I was traveling here and there for conferences, lectures, and the like. But I was inadequate at being the role model in my own home.

COVID-19 and my injury have provided the chance to reconnect with my family. This was the time that made me reflect over the fact that my family will not always be here forever. My father for example, never left behind any wealth or treasures, but he blessed us with loving memories that will last a long time in our hearts. **This made me aware to be present in their presence.** Treasure their presence, stop thinking about your work when you are at home and quit being distracted by the shiny things in life.

Pain to Gain

1. **Ask yourself if you're spending enough quality time with your family members**

   Carefully reassess if you're allotting enough time to be with them. There are a lot of people that regretted not spending enough time with their families. What would you do if you obtained what you greatly desire but you are left alone? Life is not all about the achievements and getting to the finish line but it is also about enjoying the bond of every soul that you're connected with.

2. **Carve out time to be fully present with them**

   Are you truly present where your body is? There are times that we are at home but our mind is elsewhere. If you're with your family then be fully present with them and enjoy the precious and limited moments that you have with them. Use your mobile phones if you wish, but limit the usage whenever you are around them.

3. **Reconnect the ties with other family members that are neglected**

   Initiate the connection immediately. We are oftentimes busy with other aspects of our lives that we forget to nurture the bonds of human connections. Call your relatives and have a genuine conversation with them. Check-up on them regularly because who knows when their life here on this earth will be over.

Remember, the prophet Muhammad PBUH said:

"Whosoever believes in Allah and the last day let him keep the ties of relations."
(Bukhari)

4. Don't let hate consume your relationship

Conflicts are impossible to eliminate. That's why it is essential to learn to mend the bonds and be mature enough to let go of the anger and hate when they arise. Once again, the Prophet Muhammad PBUH taught us to reconcile between ourselves when things go wrong.

Abu Darda reported: The Messenger of Allah, peace and blessings be upon him, said, "Shall I not tell you of what is better in degree than extra fasting, prayer, and charity?" They said, "Of course!"

The Prophet said, "Reconciliation between people. Verily, corrupted relations between people is the razor."
Sunan al-Tirmidhī 2509

"Do not boycott one another, do not turn away from one another, do not hate one another and do not envy one another. Be slaves of Allah, brothers.

And it is not allowed for a Muslim to avoid another for more than three days."
(al-Bukhaari, Muslim)

5. Show your appreciation to your loved ones

Even a small act should be shown appreciation. It is not the size and weight of the favors that should be measured but the intentions of people that are willingly showing you how they love and admire. Never forget to be thankful of what you received from your relationships. Because if you are not, in effect, you are not thankful to Allah SWT Himself. The prophet PBUH said:

"Whoever does not thank people has not thanked Allah."
Sunan Abī Dāwūd 4811

Remember, life's too short to dwell on things that are out of our control. Spend that time on opportunities that will help you grow and heal. Don't let the glamour of the luxurious lifestyle blind your path to true happiness and the pleasure of Allah SWT. So, treasure and maintain your bonds with others, because you are interconnected with them and can never survive without them.

Chapter Six

REALISTIC POSITIVITY

Realistic Positivity

It is a mistake to assume that life will always be smooth sailing. We often try to minimize the hardships of life and push our blind positivity to others.

You can't be everything that you want in life. It is possible that you can achieve some, but it is not a failure if you can't get it all. As humans, we should embrace who we are, our strengths and weaknesses. Do not deny your personality just because others disapprove of it. We grew up hearing various voices on how we should act and feel. We are often lost and can't find our genuine voices and thoughts.

My journey began when I started knowing who Allah SWT is. This led me to a path that is truer than before. I was no longer chasing the fame and wealth of yesterday. As a result of knowing who Allah SWT is, I started knowing who I am and what is it that I can do in life to serve my Creator.

One of the things that I discovered and loved dearly is managing teams. Leadership is one of the areas that I greatly enjoy. Not to control the masses, but to empower them where possible. So, I decided to work hard on this area to strengthen and sharpen this skill.

Imperfect perfect life

What is a perfect life? Many think that there is a certain formula for one that must be followed to achieve it. But I believe that balance should be followed throughout life. It is not enough to improve your career and always hustle. Some cultures think that dedicating all your waking hours to work is the only path to success. As Muslims however, we believe that a perfect life will only exist in the Hereafter when Allah blesses us with Paradise.

> *"Whoever does righteousness, whether male or female, while he is a believer — We will surely cause him to live a good life, and We will surely give them their reward [in the Hereafter] according to the best of what they used to do."*
> Qur'an 16:97

1. **What is a perfect life for you?**

    Think about what that would include. You should ask yourself what you value most in life. Allah? His messenger? The religion? Your family? Work? Etc. . . . Be extremely honest in answering this, not because you think that it is right but because this is your current state in life that perhaps needs a little bit of adjustment.

2. **Observe where your time is being spent**

    We can say that we value our families all day long, but do we really spend enough time with them? For example, you're a man who greatly values his family, but is often absent in important family moments. There is an inconsistency between what is seen as a priority vs. actual behavior.

Realistic Positivity

You see, if I spoke to you right now through these pages and asked you "Do you love Allah SWT?" I can almost hear your response back loud and clear: "YES." But "are you willing to follow what Allah SWT commanded?" This is the real challenge.

3. **Balance work and fun**

   A man that overloads his schedule with work is not better than one who is drowned by pleasures. We have twenty-four hours in a day, although what the media shows is that a balance in life is easily attainable. That is a dangerous lie that would pressure ourselves into thinking that we are not doing enough or not trying our best. Achieving balance requires hard work and consistency. We must be aware of how we manage our life.

   Relaxing from time to time gives our body and mind a time to recover. This would result in us having enough energy and enthusiasm for the next day.

   The delusion of eliminating the hardships of life is scary. We live in an age where everybody's highlights are easily observed with a click. This in turn creates the artificial reality that everybody is having a great time except for us. We think that their life is always paradise and that we are alone in our miseries. So here are few remedies to test out:

My Wheelchair

1. **Break the illusion, live in the reality**

    We should be aware of the message that we can achieve a stress-free life. Problems will always be present in our lives. We are not defective if we are experiencing these struggles. Inform yourself of the truth of these hidden lies of perfection. Realize that what you see is not the full story. People are manipulating what others see as a glimpse of their reality.

2. **Accept what you lack and your struggles**

    Why do you keep controlling things that are out of your control? Stop torturing yourself and accept the reality. Stop living in this illusion that you deserve a life without problems. You are not entitled to an easy life. Furthermore, your standard of an easy life is not the same as other people.

3. **Know what you can control and strive to improve it**

    On the other side, there are things that you can control. Focus on them and think carefully how this can enhance your life. For example, I could not control the progress of my recovery but I could make way for

Realistic Positivity

activities that I could do while I was in a wheelchair. As a result I was able to function, get the motivations needed to keep me going while seeking the necessary treatment to improve my physical mobility.

Benefits of realistic positivity:

a) It will shift your mindset from a negative one into a positive one
b) Lessen the frustration that you are out of control
c) Adapt a new lifestyle that is closer to reality
d) Remove the bitterness in your heart that you are a victim of life
e) Your energy would not be wasted on wishful thinking.

Focus on what you love

Life is too short to spend our time on things that do not make our soul happy.

My best friend has been saying that he hates his work for ten years now. Yet, it's been over a decade and he still stays where he has always been, i.e., the place that he hates the most. It has provided the security that he yearns for, I agree. It has provided him with financial stability which allowed him to travel throughout the world and so on, but he has never been happy doing what he does.

We spend nearly eight hours every day at work, sometimes even thinking about it while we're at home. If you hate what you're doing and still spending your limited time on earth doing what you despise then, would you regret taking a different path in life? Our hearts need to be aligned with what we're pursuing. How can our soul be nourished if we are denying what it wants?

1. **Are you happy with where you work today?**

    I'm not talking about being happy as a fleeting feeling but do you feel genuine contentment in what you're doing? Determine what part of the job makes you drained and what makes you feel energized. Observe yourself or ask people that are close to you to know if you became a better person with this job or not.

2. **What's holding you back on changing your job?**

    If you're unhappy then what's making you hold tighter to this position? Determine the fears that are preventing you from taking that leap. Get a notebook and list down the fears and what can be an alternative solution to combat them. And please don't get me wrong, I am not suggesting that you should quit your job right now without having any backup plan on mind. Continue your work, while planning the next move, if you are not in love with what you are doing currently.

Realistic Positivity

3. Know yourself

It is possible that we became insensitive to what our soul truly wants. That is what happens when you are constantly being programmed to fit society's ideal of a successful person. Try muting these voices that assume who you are not. Delve deeper on what made you happy and fulfilled as a child and in your younger years. Was it creating things, talking to other children, seeking help from others (i.e. parents) and much more? It is in these phases that you are your most authentic self — free from the chains of being normal and fitting in. Dig deeper into who you are, then align everything else to match your personality. And remember, we are Muslims, guidance has been sent to us from High, so always seek guidance form Allah SWT in order for you to reach to the most appropriate decisions.

"O Allah, verily I seek the better [of either choice] from You, by Your knowledge, and I seek ability from You, by Your power, and I ask You from Your immense bounty. For indeed You have power, and I am powerless; You have knowledge and I know not; You are the Knower of the unseen realms. O Allah, if You know that this matter is good for me with regard to my religion, my livelihood and the end of my affair then decree it for me, facilitate it for me, and grant me blessing in it. And if You know that this matter is not good for me with regard to my religion, my livelihood and the end of my affair then

My Wheelchair

turn it away from me and me from it; and decree for me better than it, wherever it may be, and make me content with it."
Al Bukhari Vol 2, Book 21, Hadith #263

See an opportunity with every problem

The common saying, "Change lemons into lemonade" is indeed a powerful one. We cannot avoid struggles, especially the ones that test our character. But I believe there is something that we can gain from every battle that we fight no matter if we lose or win.

When I was going through that pain, I thought that my life was over. My hopes started slowly fading, but I did not let my light be completely dimmed. This book is one of the things that Allah SWT guided me to create out of the chaos that I was experiencing. Who could have imagined at that time that the notes that I had by my bedside would be later used in the hope of inspiring others to cope with their struggles!

It really tested my beliefs and the lessons that I was teaching. It also increased my awareness and empathy of other people that are suffering. Although anyone can sympathize with those that are in despair, it is those that have been through hell-like situations that can taste and vividly feel for others.

So, if you're in a state that you think you cannot escape, why not think of things that you "can" do. Acts that could

Realistic Positivity

transform your situation to the opposite direction. I think that people can learn better through adversity than comfort. It is unfortunate, but true.

Think of all the impossible activities that you can't imagine doing. Always remember that you have a finite amount of time here on earth so use it wisely. Stop mourning for opportunities that don't exist in your reality. Develop an outlook of realistic positivity.

Get a mentor

If you're unsure of how to do this, just seek a mentor to guide you through the process. Don't have enough money to hire one? Well, then watch videos of your favorite mentors online. Don't have time? Trust me there is always time for what you prioritize. Do not trick your mind in believing that you don't have time.

In choosing your mentor, choose someone that is skilled in what you want to improve upon. Don't just believe the rumors and popularity but look if he speaks the language of your heart and mind. Find someone that is approachable and not arrogant. One that can be talked to like your close friend. Someone who's interested to see you free from the shackles of your pain.

When you find your mentor, go there with an empty cup. Don't let your ego and pride blind you from accessing his knowledge and experience. You are there after all to learn and gain insights, right? Set aside the fear of making mistakes and looking foolish.

Get Inspired

I'm sharing this story with the intention of inspiring others to not lose hope in their difficulties. Because Allah SWT told us in the Qur'an:

> *"For indeed, with hardship [will be] ease."*
> Qur'an 94:5

After all this book was written when I was experiencing different kinds of battles like my mental, emotional and physical well-being. If I were not to share my thoughts and agony with those that I respect and care about, that would be selfish of me. Because these same thoughts and notes are being used to help others. And if my recorded thoughts and journey could help a soul that is almost lost in despair, then I would never keep that to myself only.

That gave me a motivation to push through the everyday pain because I knew that one day it will be worth it, especially if I could help those who are in dire need of guidance.

Share to the world who you are. Don't be ashamed of your struggles as a mortal living in this world. You never know — your journey could also save those who are in need of inspiration.

Chapter Seven

CONTENTMENT

Contentment

There is no such thing as being too comfortable in life. After all, life is full of ups and downs. So, prepare yourself to struggle and have your faith in God Almighty being tested.

I was scheduled to attend a massive peace conference in Mindanao City in the Philippines. And after the tour was over, we ended up in Manila for the final round of the conference. And the theme of the event was titled *"contentment."*

That night, before flying out to Manila, I had a very scary dream concerning my son. As it is discouraged in Islam to narrate disturbing dreams, I am keeping it to myself. I know you are curious to know, but this is not what I wanted to focus on here. All you need to know for now is that I was very disturbed by this dream and never told anyone about it when I woke up.

When we landed in Manila, the organization manager took us for lunch. The driver told me to leave my backpack and assured me that it was safe to do so because the place was surrounded by compounds and security. I had no doubt to distrust the advice, so I left my bag and went for lunch with other guests.

After about twenty minutes or so, I saw the driver crying outside the restaurant! When I went up to him, he said that somebody had broken into the car and my backpack was missing!

My Wheelchair

The bag on that day had almost everything valuable that I owned. Some cash, my laptop, iPad and most importantly **my passport**.

I was distraught as I also lost all my work, lesson notes, and had no other backup. I was left with useless information that I knew I couldn't use. Gratefully, my wife had her passport and the children's so they didn't need to worry about getting stuck in Manila like me.

The brothers around me there kindly reported the incident and told me to head to the hotel and get ready for the conference. As I left, I told my friend, *Mufti Ismael Menk*, who was also part of the conference, about my dream. And reflecting over what I had seen, we interpreted it as God Almighty taking something else from me that is insignificant instead of my precious son's life. While at that moment I was blinded by the anger of what I've lost, I took a bath to compose myself. As I looked into the pants that I was wearing, behold, I found my lecture notes about contentment that I was about to deliver that night. It made me realize that I need to make peace with myself and let God Almighty be in control of whatever happened. Otherwise, I don't deserve to stand on that stage and teach people about contentment.

I started reflecting over the possibility that God Almighty could have taken something precious like my son's life and so, I should be thankful that we are all safe. The things that I lost at the time were easily replaceable, unlike my loved

Contentment

ones. I proceeded to attend my event and guess what? The opening statement of my speech was the story of losing my backpack. I even joked about being *"passport-less"* and was finally calm and contented with my situation.

I said *"Alhamdulillah"*, all praises are due to God Almighty for what He had destined. And I brought my family members together that night, including my son who was crying for losing some of his items in the incident. And I told them to accept whatever happened and be thankful that we are safe and still together. I assured them that all material possessions are easily replaceable by Allah's grace and permission and so, let's move on.

My talk was about contentment so I should demonstrate this myself despite the situation, right? It was like a direct trial of what I was going to teach. My introduction to the topic was my story. I narrated my situation while laughing about being *stateless* and everybody was laughing along with me. I also told them that I'm unsure of how to return to Hong Kong and China where I lived and when I will reunite once again with my family.

Yes, it was a very sad situation the next morning. It was the time for my flight back home, but instead, I was left behind in the Philippines while my family went back safely to China.

I was really frustrated at first. But I now realized that it was Allah's plan for me to stay there for a while.

My Wheelchair

I was stuck in the Philippines for a while because the Egyptian embassy in Manila was too slow to issue a new passport for me. A friend of mine, *Yusuf Valdez* and his wife *Jannah* let me stay at their house for three months or more. I was a bit shy and worried that my stay might cause inconvenience, but soon enough, I was able to understand more clearly why things happened the way they happened.

> *"You may dislike something although it is good for you, or like something, although it is bad for you."*
> Qur'an 2:216

Had it not been for what had happened, I would've never been able to roam the country and organize more events during this period. It was good in a way that I was able to spread the teaching of Islam and witness hundreds of people benefiting. The only downside was that I missed my family so much, although my wife visited me from Hong Kong twice.

Here are a few insights that have benefited me from the above experience and its connection to what I went through during these months of being wheelchair bound.

Ar Rida — Contentment/satisfaction

We should not attempt to be in control of everything that we want in life. Not everything can be changed just because we want it to.

Contentment

The division between inner peace and contentment is acceptance of negative situations that are happening in our lives. The moment you accept and move on is the moment you will feel the calmness in your heart. ***Change the things that can be and let things that can't be just be.***

My legs were numb and I couldn't change that. Although the doctors said that my condition can improve in the long run through surgery then later exercise and physiotherapy. But I put the focus on the things that I had control over.

Just like in my situation, there are things in life that simply can't be forced or altered. And, as humans we want to regain control of our lives. We want the power to manipulate things and events to work out the way we want. But reality operates differently. We should accept that some situations and circumstances are just out of our reach. So, here are a few points that could help you when things go against your will.

Ask yourself what are the things that you want to change?
Evaluate if some of what you've listed can be changed by you?
Let go of the feeling that you need to be always in control.
Shift your focus on what you can change and improve about your situation.
Stop blaming yourself for having no control of your destiny. It is in the Hands of Allah SWT.

My Wheelchair

Sakinah — Calmness

> "We certainly belong to Allah,
> and to Him we are bound to return."
> Qur'an 2:156

We need to remind ourselves that Allah SWT has a plan for us. You may view it as an unlucky fate but He knows what's better for you. How many times have we questioned why certain things are happening to us? But did we ask the question, is it really for me to decide anything?

Struggles come in your life for a reason; to make you stronger and test your faith in Allah SWT. Don't expect to remove all the hardships that are currently present. You are not entitled to a heaven-like life while you are still living here on earth. So be patient and wait for Him to show you the exit out of your difficulties. And if the difficulties persisted, then expect a greater life in Jannah — Paradise.

I urge you to pray consistently despite the ups and downs of life. Stop making conditions that you'll pray only if good things are happening. Don't ever be a conditional believer, don't be like the people described in the below verses:

> *"It is He who enables you to travel on land and sea until, when you are in ships and they sail with them by a good wind and they rejoice therein,* **there comes a storm wind and the waves come upon them from everywhere and they assume that they are surrounded, supplicating**

Contentment

Allah, sincere to Him in religion, 'If You should save us from this, we will surely be among the thankful.'

But when He saves them, at once they commit injustice upon the earth without right. O mankind, your injustice is only against yourselves, [being merely] the enjoyment of worldly life. Then to Us is your return, and We will inform you of what you used to do."
Qur'an 10:22-23

Lastly, if you think that Allah SWT prevents you from having certain things in life, it is absolutely for your own good. You may not understand it for now but there is a greater purpose behind these events. For example, He may be not letting you have that kind of fame that you desire as He knows that you are not ready to be in the spotlight. You may have an ego problem that may blind you and giving you fame would worsen your character.

So, how to face these calamities with calmness?

1. Don't let your anger and frustrations make you forget your prayers.
2. Accept your destiny written and planned by your Creator.
3. Wait for God Almighty's answers while praying devoutly.
4. Make Du'a, Supplicate consistently.
5. Don't resent God's plan for you as the Qadar/destiny of Allah SWT is always good.

Tama'ninah — Tranquility

Sheik Abu Ishaq Al Heweny, one of the most respected scholars of Hadith (*narrations of Prophet Muhammad*), discussed his amputated leg in an interview on TV sometime ago. When he was asked about his level of tranquility and contentment regarding what happened to him, he said that he has good hope in Allah SWT that his leg had preceded him to *Jannah*. Despite the fact that his leg had been amputated, he remained composed, faithful, and peaceful.

How many of us can maintain their calmness when a misfortune happens? I really admire his positive outlook on life and His hope in Allah's mercy and rewards despite his adversity.

There will come a time that you will experience an event so painful that it will consume your peace within. Remember, that there are those that have greater suffering yet they still maintain their calmness and faith. So praise Allah SWT, for your trials could've been worse.

Tawakul — Reliance on Allah SWT

Remember this: for every calamity that threatens your sanity, Allah SWT is well aware of it. So, pray, and pray harder, but also bear in mind that your actions are required to bring about some positive changes in your life. This is basically the concept of *Tawakul*. One of the narrations that I really love is when the Prophet Muhammad PBUH said:

Contentment

"If you all depend on Allah with due reliance, He would certainly give you provision as He gives it to birds who go forth hungry in the morning and return with full belly at dusk."
Riyad as-Salihin 79

He provides to the birds, only when they fly and do their part in search for provisions. Had they remained in their nests hoping to be fed, they would have died of hunger.

The Prophet Ibrahim PBUH, one day decided to destroy the idols in his town. He took an initiative to awaken people and remind them that nothing has the right to be worshipped except Allah SWT.

Once they found out what he did, they planned a punishment for him. They made the decision to construct a furnace, set it on fire and literally burn him. They were not playing around; they proceeded with their plan and threw him in a blazing fire. But Ibrahim PBUH remained calm, knowing that he had completed his mission and did all that Allah SWT had commanded Him to do. As a result, God Almighty intervened, instructed the fire to be cool and safe upon Ibrahim PBUH.

The fire symbolized the tests and trials that we may face in life. So long as you are doing what Allah SWT had commanded, don't worry, trials will come your way, but soon they will fade away as a result of your patience and faith in Allah SWT.

My Wheelchair

Ibrahim PBUH, on another occasion, went on a mission to deliver the message of Allah SWT and left behind his wife *Hajar* and his son *Ismail* PBUH in an open desert. Hajar didn't make sense of what was happening as Ibrahim PBUH couldn't explain clearly why he was leaving. When she asked him if Allah had commanded him to do this, and he replied in the affirmative, she immediately responded that Allah SWT will never abandon her and her child.

She was left behind with an infant, but she had faith that would later become her aid to cope with one of the hardest challenges in human history. She had to run several times between the two hills of *Safa* and *Marwa* because she was heartbroken to see her son in pain out of hunger and thirst. She relied on Allah SWT fully, yet she did what she can to save her child and as a result, Zamzam water flowed from between her son's feet to quench their thirst and respond to *Hajar's* solid and unshakable faith.

These two stories demonstrate how having complete trust in Allah's plan can make you survive situations that are even deadly. Don't doubt what Allah SWT has planned for you and don't question His intentions. Your job is to worship Him and work hard to establish His religion on earth.

Remember, Allah SWT is your maker, He knows better than you know yourself. All these tests and trials that you will experience are a way to know if you will stick to your convictions or not. Think about your current dilemma at the

Contentment

moment. Do you have complete trust that God will provide for you as He provides for all His creation?

You may be thinking that you have the most difficult problem of all people. And will justify your hopelessness with being a victim of all the things that are happening. Be honest with yourself, does this do you any good or does this make your situation worse?

I suggest you look at the blessings in your life and count them instead of focusing on the problems. Avoid the blame game and take responsibility for your situation. You will learn a lot by self-reflection. Pointing the finger at someone else or something that had happened in your life will only make you feel that you've escaped accountability for your own problems. It is just simply a quick fix to your suffering, but never a solution.

A long-term solution would be accepting your destiny and changing things that you can manage and have control over. Pray consistently no matter what life throws at you and finally, believe that Allah SWT only wants what's best for you and that He is not after your misery.

> "... and Allah wants no injustice to the worlds."
> Qur'an 3:108

> *"Allah intends for you ease and does not intend for you hardship..."*
> Qur'an 2:185

My Wheelchair

"Allah wants to make clear to you [the lawful from the unlawful] and guide you to the [good] practices of those before you and to accept your repentance. And Allah is Knowing and Wise."

Qur'an 4:26

Chapter Eight

STRETCH

Stretch

Limits. A well-known concept reminding us of where we can only go.

For those who are afraid of pushing themselves beyond their comfort zones, then probably you'll need to hear how I was able, by Allah's aid, to overcome this stage even when the odds appeared to be stacked against me.

Two people in particular need to be mentioned here since they had a significant influence on me. Although I had numerous mentors throughout my life, these two stood out as the most relatable in terms of pushing themselves to new heights despite physical limitations and other challenges. They are Nick Vujicic the author of *Life Without Limits* and Muhammad Ali, probably the greatest boxer of all time. During my darkest days of pain and severe weakness, they've inspired me to push past all my boundaries and get up back on my feet.

Nick Vujicic is an Australian man who was born without limbs: no legs or arms. A person that we may describe as "disabled" and "incapable" due to his physical limitations. Such a *"disabled"* man is able to surf the water, swim without limbs, inspire millions around the world to cope with life challenges, author best-selling books and achieve so much more. One could never imagine that such ability exists in what we label, wrongly, as "disability."

Although I had read his works prior to my accident, re-reading them had a very different impact on me. I was

My Wheelchair

able to decipher his messages with more clarity and with a direction and a roadmap in mind. And that includes how to practically function in the society with the ability that I CAN create for myself. Nick, despite all the odds and the questions that we have in mind about HOW in the world he was able to accomplish all of what he did, focused on himself, and in doing so, was able to inspire millions around the world.

He conveys the idea that there are no excuses for not pursuing your dreams. Consider what it would be like to be born without any of your arms or legs. Just try it out and tie your hands right now and try to live normally. How will that look like? Are you now grateful for what you already have?

Would you be miserable if you knew your body or any of its parts became limited?

It is up to us whether we choose to blame and curse everything in life as a result of what we may face or decide to make our journey worthwhile by believing in our ability to overcome obstacles and grow as individuals.

Muhammad Ali was regarded as one of the greatest boxers of his era, and possibly, of all time. He was also a social activist at the time, fighting for the rights of black Americans and speaking courageously against injustice of all sorts. The man who would speak so fast as a result of his sharp brain, intelligence and passion. That same man was struck with Parkinson's disease which impacted his mobility and speech.

He once mentioned that he was tested by this disease to be always reminded that he is NOT the Greatest, rather, God is. He saw it as a test of his humility and patience. He did not sit back rejoicing over the memories of the old days, he resumed to inspire the world through his appearances on national and international TVs, writing books, sharing his experience and wisdom and encouraging others to become the best versions of themselves.

These two individuals were one of the reasons why I decided to write this book. So perhaps, those who are suffering from any sort of pain, would regain their strength and get back up on their feet and live up to their potential.

If Ali and Nick were able to defeat their challenges, then what's stopping me from doing the things I enjoy while in my wheelchair? And what could possibly stop you from doing the same? Don't succumb to your situation with hopelessness. Rather, maintain a positive outlook on life and keep stretching your limits.

The lessons that follow are based on the Stretch concept.

Take charge of your life

Are you giving up on your life? I know that it is easier to quit and do nothing when you're experiencing struggles and loss. But time is still passing and we don't have unlimited chances of living. Pause for a second and ask yourself if you're

My Wheelchair

doing yourself a favor by wallowing in your problems. It is also indeed easy to make up excuses on why you "can't" do it.

> *"And who despairs of the mercy of his*
> *Lord except for those astray?"*
> Qur'an 15:56

So, giving up on yourself will increase your misguidance in this world and in the Hereafter as well. Because you have lost hope in the One who could reverse your situation.

We mistake being too dependent as a good way to live when in reality it never is. Being passive won't improve your life as you let others have the steering wheel to your fate. Yes, bad things may happen in your life but is it worth it to stop moving forward?

While suffering from my illness, I wanted to do something that I could easily manage. Hence, I took charge and made ways to fulfill my dreams. I contacted the school and let them know of my condition. They were kind enough to accommodate my needs, to an extent that my office door was redesigned to allow a sufficient amount of space for my wheelchair to move in and out without any hazard or difficulty.

But as I returned to my job, people started to advise me to just rest, take it easy, we will do it for you and the like. I knew that they only had good intentions while saying this. In all honesty, I didn't want to hear any of that, because I didn't want to believe that I am incapable of performing my duties.

Stretch

Being passive is all about making yourself the victim of your circumstances and surrendering to the challenge you are facing. But the question is, is that truly living or merely existing? And so, I took charge of my own situation. I had assessed my limitations, so I knew when to rest and when to keep the wheel running. Instead of burdening others with MY tasks, I took responsibility and accountability of my outcomes. So, look at your current state and determine who is in hold of the steering wheel?

Like some of you, I've been told that my condition was a hopeless case and I'll never know when it will improve. I was reminded that it would take a long time and many resources to get better. And so, I allowed myself a time to heal, I refused to limit myself to the wheelchair, so I trained my weakest leg until it responded to me. You see, I took charge of my own situation.

To get things done, it requires the consistency of trying again and again even if no results are being observed. I believe that I can do it and will see the results in the long term. Motivating oneself in this time needs a mind that can fight those self-doubts and negative thoughts that are pulling you away from your goal. So, in brief, what is it that you need to do?

1. Assess if you're taking charge of your life.
2. Determine the limits that are being imposed upon you.
3. Change your mindset from passive to active.

4. Train yourself to surpass those limits in place.
5. Be consistent in the change that you want to see in your life.

Stretch as far as you can

All of us are born with a different set of abilities and disabilities. It is very important to be honest with yourself about these traits. You should not compare what you're given with others' gifts and talents as that would only result in envy and bitterness. Instead of comparing, why not be inspired by the uniqueness of each individual.

Learn from those who are very different from you. If your strongest ability is to mentor others then use this to improve other people's lives. Don't be stuck on putting too much energy into your disabilities. For example, if I allotted more focus on my illness then how could I be where I'm at right now, on my feet?

There's a purpose behind why each of us is blessed with different skill sets and weaknesses, and that is the fact that we need each other. It does not make you less of a person if you ask for help from others to fill the gaps of your weaknesses. You could in turn share your abilities with others and help them the way you would want to receive assistance. So ask yourself:

1. What are your abilities and weaknesses?

2. Think about your abilities and how you will use them.
3. Collaborate with those that are strong in the areas of your weakness.

Make great decisions

Life is not a race to see who's going to make it first. I think it is a journey that each of us have to experience and arrive at our own pace. I was moving on from a state of hopelessness to a stage of acceptance. I got all the help I needed to walk again but my pace was not that fast.

Sometime back, at the end of the school academic year, teachers and staff organized a small version of *The Amazing Race* on campus. I was staring at the event sadly knowing that I won't be able to participate with my condition. But my colleagues insisted that I should take part in the event and so they started pushing my wheelchair around and we truly had a lot of fun. Even though, I made it to the finish line last, I was able to complete all stages of the race. For me, that was the most important part of the day.

I once thought that life was meant to be lived and enjoyed by the fastest and the strongest to reach those social expectations like wealth and fame. But those areas are temporary and will never last forever. Some of us go through life in a fast-paced manner and forget to stop by and enjoy life's natural wonders. We are not ranked by our speed, and our worth is not determined by who gets there faster.

Cherish the process of getting better. The journey is there for you to appreciate the process of being a better version of yourself. Even when life throws at you struggles that would make you stop for a while, continue going on with faith in Allah SWT to ease your pain and allow you to bear the dramas. You know in your heart that you will get there just by slowly moving forward. So do yourself a favor and . . .

1. Don't compare your pace with others.
2. Move forward even if you are slow.
3. Cherish the journey and the process to arrive where you want to.
4. If you encounter setbacks just keep pushing through.

Grow in knowledge

Our brains are very powerful in deciding what we do in our everyday lives from the moment we wake up to the time we rest. Yes, we are born as blank slates in this world, and by interacting with others we learn the information necessary to understand how this world works. Allah SWT states:

> "And Allah has extracted you from the wombs of your mothers not knowing a thing, and He made for you hearing and vision and intellect that perhaps you would be grateful."
> Qur'an 16:78

But not all information stored is useful and beneficial. That's why the Prophet Muhammad PBUH was constantly asking Allah SWT to grant him beneficial knowledge, not just any knowledge.

Whenever my mind was dragging me down to moments of depression and fear, reading books and listening to online lectures were my remedy to get back to reality and focus on the way ahead of me.

Reading books is not just a hobby meant for entertaining ourselves, but it can be a source of life-changing wisdom that could alter our lives for the better. There are many people before you who have gone through the same or similar challenge. Do not try to reinvent the wheel, read about how they were able to utilize their challenge and reverse the situation in their favor.

One of the books that was always by my bedside during these painful days was the biography of the Prophet Muhammad PBUH. Despite being the prophet of God who has been chosen by the Creator Himself to deliver the message of Islam, he too struggled a lot throughout the journey of his mission as a prophet. He lost all his children during his lifetime except one, he saw his beloved companions dying and being tortured by the disbelievers of Mecca, he was beaten up during one of the battles and was bleeding all over his face, he lost his beloved wife and uncle in the most critical time of his life, yet he came out of this struggle as victorious, praised and successful, and that's because he was patient and always connected with Allah SWT.

In Chapter Ninety-three of the Qur'an, Allah SWT comforted the Prophet Muhammad PBUH when he was visiting the people of Ta'ef to invite them to Islam but sadly, he was greeted with harsh treatment by people, including children stoning him and the companion who was with him. They had to run out of the town to save their lives.

The angels were sent by Allah SWT to the Prophet PBUH seeking his permission to crush and bury the people of Ta'ef and the entire town alive. He, PBUH said "no" he'd rather be patient, hoping that one of their descendants will one day worship Allah alone. Even on the bitterest day of his life, he displayed patience and prayed for his enemies. As distressful as you can imagine going through this experience was, he made the following Du'a/supplication:

> *"Oh Allah, I complain to You my weakness, my lack of resources, and my lowliness before men. Oh the Most Merciful! You are the Lord of the weak and You are my Lord. To whom will You relinquish my fate! To an enemy who will misuse me? Or to a closed person whom You have given power over me?* ***If You are not angry with me then I care not what happens to me.*** *Your favour is all that counts for me."*

Going through these lessons from the life of the most beloved of Allah's creation, brought peace and patience

Stretch

into my heart and soul and made me overlook my problem. These narratives and more, are a collection of human beings who demonstrated patience despite the hardships they have experienced and how trusting Allah SWT and expecting the reward from Him was the solution to cope with these severe challenges. So read . . .

Fight every day, fight till the end. Even if you die at the battle, people will remember you with dignity and honor. Meaning that you've fought to change your life to the better and didn't allow passivity to be part of who you are.

Yes, we all should be aware of our limits but also should not be scared of it. Gather your courage to mould that limit and make a new path to your progress. Make wise decisions that will be consistent with the change that you're aiming for. And lastly, keep on seeking the knowledge that will give you the wisdom to navigate the hardships and pain in life.

Chapter Nine

LOSERS GIVE UP, WINNERS GIVE VALUE

Losers Give Up, Winners Give Value

Is there a time when you wanted to give up everything because of what you are going through? Well, let me tell you that Allah SWT will put you to the test with many obstacles to come, and the route you're on will never be completely smooth. It will get easier, but the roughness will never cease to exist.

There was a voice in my head telling me to give up while I was going through that ordeal. It was as if I was hurting myself in the hopes of being able to walk again. But there were two things that kept me going and fighting these thoughts: my love for my family and my passion to inspire others.

Let's take a look at where you are now in your life. If you've ever desired to end all of your troubles and misery, I hope this will help you continue on your quest Insh a Allah/ God willing. Ask yourself, aside from worshipping Allah SWT as the ultimate purpose of your existence, what is your life's purpose that you would like to achieve? What are the activities that will keep you motivated in good times and during the bad ones as well? Think deeply then write them down.

The majority of us have dreams and ambitions that we want to realize. It all comes down to whether you want to continue or give up. It is no one's responsibility but yourself.

After attending a *John Maxwell* lecture in which he remarked, *"Losers give up, winners impart values,"* I got the idea for this chapter. I truly believe that if you persevere, you will gain essential life lessons and the necessary insights to pass them on to others as well.

Bethany Hamilton, who is a very competitive surfer in America despite losing her arm at the age of thirteen due to a shark attack, was an inspiration for me to write this chapter. She could have easily given up her dream and become afraid of the ocean, but following her recovery, she returned to surf the big waves with only one arm and continued to be optimistic, believing that God had a good reason for all that had happened. After the tragedy, she continued to train and won several competitions in in the sport that she loved the most. Surfing.

What if she had given up her dream in exchange for the loss of her arm? She may have regretted it until this day. And if that had happened, she probably would have become angry at herself and her heart would have never forgiven her. Her current self, however, is proud of her belief in her ability to surf again. And she continues to live that dream to this day.

If you find that inspiring just like me, then you could also search for your role models who demonstrate the persistence needed to overcome their struggles. Study how they view their struggles and illnesses and how they were able to function and become productive despite their difficulties. You would have a clue on interpreting your own battles in life. This could make you hold on longer when you want to just give up. Allah SWT said in the Qur'an:

Losers Give Up, Winners Give Value

> *"And these examples We present to the people that perhaps they will give thought."*
> Qur'an 59:21

Here are the lessons that I wanted to teach everyone about never giving up on life. Don't skim these words but rather digest them, slowly absorbing the insights that I have gained during these painful days.

Never despair

If you have been in despair or are going through it then you know the emptiness that you feel in your heart. It's like you've become blinded to the opportunities and possibilities that life offers through the bounties and mercy of Allah SWT. All you see is the darkness that you're going to be a failure or your existence is meaningless. You also feel that you're alone with these emotions and nobody cares about you. But let me just remind you of one of the most hopeful verses of the entire Qur'an, perhaps these words will get you back up on your feet.

> *Say, "O My servants who have transgressed against themselves [by sinning], do not despair of the mercy of Allah. Indeed, Allah forgives all sins. Indeed, it is He who is the Forgiving, the Merciful."*
> Qur'an 39:53

My Wheelchair

Why would you give up on yourself if Allah SWT Himself is not giving up on you?

When we do wrong, we are not harming other people but we are really hurting ourselves. So *"do not despair from the mercy of Allah."* If things go the opposite of what you want, don't worry because Allah SWT can always fix your affairs provided that you maintain your sanity and faith in Him.

This verse lifted me up every time that I was in despair. And I hope that it would do the same for you. Otherwise, I am afraid that you will be placed in the categories of the faithless ones. Allah said:

> *"And who despairs of the mercy of his Lord except for those astray?"*
> Qur'an 15:56

The non-believers don't have someone that they can rely upon. If things get worse, they easily fall into despair. They may view their struggles as something that is within their control but in most cases they can't handle it. This will make them more hopeless of their situation and as a result, many may choose to end their own lives.

But you, as a believer, it is absolutely necessary to strengthen your faith in Allah SWT, your Creator. This would lessen the burden that you're fighting this battle on your own. The truth is you could not go through life alone let alone if challenges appear. Stop pretending that you can take care of it yourself. You can never be at peace for pretending to be a strong individual that needs no one. We all need Allah SWT more than ever to survive these painful moments.

I recommend you find the answers in the Qur'an especially if you're feeling despair. Be inspired by the stories and lessons embedded in this amazing book of guidance. Relate it with what you're going through in your own life. Write notes and reflections of the specific parts that resonate with you and do your best to implement what you can.

You need to examine what's causing your despair. Is it because of what you did or something that is done by others? Carefully observe what kind of thoughts are going through your mind. Talk to a trusted adult about it or write it in your journal and if you are still struggling with your thoughts, please seek help from professionals.

Above all, be honest of the current state of your faith in Allah SWT. Be open to admitting if it's increasing or decreasing in your current situation. Know why this happened and find ways to bring back the hope and reliance on Allah SWT to your heart. There's no strength better than having faith in Allah SWT.

Never doubt yourself

I was scared that I was going to lose it all due to my condition. These kinds of thoughts would make me doubt myself. What if I can't do this? What if I'm forever in this condition? These gushing negative thoughts were always dragging me down and preventing me from progressing.

The change started when I changed my mindset, and focused on creating what I CAN DO. Getting real with myself that I am still the same *Wael* with less motion but with a creative mind and loads of productivity and things that I would love to achieve. Starting from there, I gathered the courage again to create something of value that perhaps will become my legacy after departing this world.

Instead of wasting my time and life on negative thoughts I did things that I could do.

I continued to work even while I was in my wheelchair. I felt no annoyance in narrating my painful story to my students and colleagues anymore, in fact, I was told that the story was so inspiring. *Alhamdulilah*/all praises due to Allah SWT alone.

I remember when I was invited to record thirty episodes on Huda TV which were aired later on and generated a lot of interest. I remember how much pain was hitting me all over my waist but it subsided the moment I would speak with passion during the episodes. That happened because my time was spent wisely once I started dealing with reality. That was achieved when I believed in my ability that I can do it.

Losers Give Up, Winners Give Value

How can you achieve your dreams and goals if you yourself can't see it happening? You are your first cheerleader every time that you're facing those doubts. It is your responsibility to gently remind yourself of your strengths and gifts that you could share with others.

Yes, there will also be those that doubt you but it all starts with yourself. What kind of stories are you telling yourself? Determine if it is mostly things that you can do, rather than those that are beyond your abilities.

Most of the time when I mentioned what I've been through at school, I would get these looks of "how in the world were you able to do that?" In my perspective, they couldn't believe that it is possible for some people to overcome their struggles. It is indeed easy to become passive about what is happening to you. It is more difficult to battle these struggles and still come out optimistic about life. But I knew, despite all the difficulties and hurdles, that I could still follow my dreams and goals of serving my family members and other people as well.

Not doubting yourself comes with many benefits, and one of those is you get to try what you deem impossible before. Time is passing and worrying won't produce any results. It is better to believe in yourself and take that leap. You may end up with failure after failure but you won't be burdened by what ifs anymore. In fact, you won't even regret or blame yourself for not doing your best and exhorting all possible avenues.

It is amazing to instill the courage to trust one's self. There would be possibilities of getting to know yourself better and what you are good at. And you could also, in the long run, easily believe in the potential of other people as well, and that's because you've started with yourself.

Never regret

When I had my second painful disc in my lower left side, I regretted it a lot. I held myself responsible and at fault because I pushed myself to wear my pants while standing. It was after this day that I wasn't able to feel anything in my right leg from the knee down. At first, I blamed myself so much. But I was also reminded that God Almighty has decided it and so it happened.

> *"Indeed, Allah does what He intends."*
> Qur'an 22:14

I've come to a realization that the past has already passed and it's gone forever. And we can't rewind the past to choose something different. I knew that I needed to move on. And so, what if it was my fault? Aren't we human beings and we usually make mistakes? If it was my mistake, I admit it and I should learn from the experience and move on. I should now focus on recovery until I get better but I will not go back and torture myself for what has happened. We believe in the *Qadar* of Allah SWT or destiny, therefore we should not regret anything. Allah SWT said:

Losers Give Up. Winners Give Value

> "And there is not a thing but that with Us are its depositories, and We do not send it down except according to a known measure."
> Qur'an 15:21

So, if you are constantly retracing what you have done wrong in the past, stop it. You can't change the past but you can do something about your present and future. Quit those regrets that you could have chosen another option. Move on and take accountability for your current actions.

Never doubt Allah SWT

Why do we question our Creator for the calamities and trials that are happening to us? Never think that God Almighty is punishing you for what's going on in your life. He is testing you and your level of faith in Him. Your true character will show in these hard times whether it is good or not. Moreover, you must remember that these trials become a means of reward once you've demonstrated patience. So why assume the worst?

If you want to know if Allah SWT is punishing you or rewarding you, look at your actions and see if they are in line with what Allah SWT has commanded or not. If they are, then it is a reward to elevate your status in Jannah Insh a Allah. We're informed that the agony we feel when we're in a bad situation is expiation of prior misdeeds. The Prophet Muhammad PBUH said:

My Wheelchair

> *"Never a believer is stricken with a discomfort, an illness, an anxiety, a grief or mental worry or even the pricking of a thorn but Allah will expiate his sins on account of his patience."*
> Al Bukhari & Muslim - Riyad as-Salihin 37

These lessons will remind you that you should not give up on your path. The darkness is not permanent, you could let the light in if you open it up by yourself. Just ask yourself the question, how much do you trust Allah SWT and yourself?

Evaluate your situation if you're feeling hopeless to continue with your journey. Stop letting yourself suffer endlessly about events that have happened in the past. Take care of your present and future and learn to move on. Perseverance and beautiful patience will lead you to an amazing reward in the Hereafter and will inspire others to do the same.

Chapter Ten

INSPIRE OTHERS

Inspire Others

This book was created mainly to comfort and inspire those that are in the same state. It is my hope that it will touch the souls that are going through similar challenges or have tasted the feeling of hopelessness.

With a lot of pain and suffering around the world, this goal became my reason to be inspired and motivated every single day. Even though I'm still recovering to date, I realized that the world does not revolve around me. So "let's do the work" was my slogan. I started going online, posting videos, speaking honestly about my struggles, using my wheelchair without being ashamed, because I needed to normalize the life that Allah SWT had given me after my injury.

As a result, I was received with acceptance and not criticism. Although, at first, I was feeling that they're only having pity whenever they see me. But now I have a different narrative. People usually get inspired when they see through your authentic self. They don't value words and slogans unless you've lived them and practically have experienced them. Seeing that kept me going with creating content even though I was not in my best condition.

One day, I woke up and found myself making a vow that I will create this book in the year 2021–2022. I also posted this announcement online to keep myself reminded of that promise. Not only that, but people online started making me accountable for this goal. In reality, writing a book is no easy task as it requires the hard work and consistency to share your deepest thoughts and emotions. My vision was to make something that could help those who are in need and in search of contentment and rest in the middle of challenges that seem so hard to bear.

Did it ever occur to you that you could be an inspiration to others? Look at your experiences in the past, there may be someone that could find those useful, to shed a light on their own painful struggles. Like what happened to me may seem an unlucky fate by others, but my perspective is different. There must be a purpose why God Almighty intended this to happen.

> *"And Allah Knows, while you know not."*
> Qur'an 2:216

He knows that I can withstand the battles and hardships that come my way. I also want you to know that having this confidence in Him is really possible. It is time to leave our focus on our own misery and redirect it in motivating others to be enlightened. Will you show your perseverance to help those in need? The Prophet Muhammad PBUH reminded us of this great and noble deed.

> *"A Muslim is a brother of (another) Muslim, he neither wrongs him nor does hand him over to one who does him wrong. If anyone fulfills his brother's needs, Allah will fulfill his needs; if one relieves a Muslim of his troubles, Allah will relieve his troubles on the Day of Resurrection; and if anyone covers up a Muslim (his sins), Allah will cover him up (his sins) on the Resurrection Day."*
> Al Bukhari & Muslim - Riyad as-Salihin 244

Inspire Others

The lessons in this chapter are not the end of your journey. Reflecting and comparing it to your life experience will bring you the clarity that you're looking for. This guide may not fit perfectly with you but the information can help you decide to have a life that is more purposeful and peaceful.

Share your life's painful moments

Most of society's teachings are not revealing the ugly parts of your life. This belief that we should only show the moments wherein we are at our happiest is very damaging. After all, you can't have a life without the painful moments otherwise, that would be an unrealistic standard to uphold and could lead to a depressive outcome. We may use different tactics to hide the bad but the truth will always prevail in the long run. And please, don't get me wrong. I am not suggesting, in any way, that a person should broadcast his or her sinful activities, but to share the side that can uplift others who are lost is absolutely beneficial. Just like how Ja'far Ibn Abee Talib RA did when he met An Najashi, the King of Ethiopia at that time. When the King asked him "what did your Prophet PBUH teach you?" he said:

> *"O King! we were plunged in the depth of ignorance and barbarism; we adored idols, we lived unchastely, we ate the meat, and we spoke abominations, we disregarded every feeling of humanity, and the duties of hospitality*

My Wheelchair

and neighborhood were neglected; we knew no law but that of the strong..."
[Reference: Ar-Raheeq Al-Makhtum]

The narration of Ja'far was the inspirational arrow that hits everyone who listened to his speech on that day. Was he exposing his sins? Absolutely not. But sometimes, your past painful moments could become the most uplifting and life-changing for others.

Also, it is not advisable to present yourself to the world as a perfect being. First, you're lying to yourself because we are not perfect, we do have our shortcomings and ugly history. Secondly, people won't be able to relate to you, therefore, you won't be able to make any impact on others and lastly, you will start losing touch with reality and believe yourself.

Stop spreading these delusions that your life is like a fairy tale that is always going so smoothly. You're not helping yourself or others in any form, rather you're robbing them of the opportunity of learning and changing for the better. How can people be inspired by you if they can't have the connection that you're just a human like them.

Yes, I'm one of the teachers of faith but it does not mean that I should be perfect 24/7 without falling short. I'm human just like the rest of you and I admit my weaknesses and mistakes that I've made. I don't have to share vivid details but I am allowed to share enough to lift you up and inspire you as much as I can. Nobody should be forced to be perfect or pretend that things are okay while he or she are in troubles. So be yourself.

Sharing your troubles and challenges could help a person fight their own. Your story may be the push that they need to take the initiative in controlling their lives. Your hardships are not going to waste because you've gained values that you could share with others.

You don't need to be stingy with what you know and learn. Doing this would benefit no one and you could have regrets of hoarding it all to yourself someday. Instead, go out of your comfort zone and explore the ways that you could spread your wisdom to the world. It is not up to you to decide if what you shared is useful or not. The people around you will be the ones to know if it can help with their struggles or not.

The important thing is you've taken the risk to share your story. You may be fearing that this side of who you are could be perceived negatively but worry not because you know deep inside that your intentions are good and wanted nothing but to help others. People may have various reactions towards what you say or do. Not everyone will agree with you, so consult, be prepared for all scenarios, and rely on Allah SWT.

Share your strategies

I admit that there were times that I was doubting myself if I could really finish this book or get out of my constant sad mode. After all, quitting is more comfortable than persevering. But I have my purpose and motivation already set in. It really gave me the boost to finish what I've started no matter what happens.

If ever a conflict arises like pain making me suffer severely then I'm prepared to think of ways to reach my goal continuously. For example, if I can't go to conferences and seminars, I will record myself talking about the values that I wanted to share then I will post them online. Also, if I am loaded with tasks and don't have enough time, then I will make time for productivity and remove the distractions that are hindering my growth.

In inspiring those who are close to me, I will prioritize family. I've learned in this pandemic that they mean so much to me. I wanted to inspire them and be their mentor if they are experiencing any challenge in life. Your family are mostly the first ones to notice if you're being an inspiration to others. Because if you didn't inspire them, your inspiration to others is meaningless. So, prioritize your family members.

You can develop the necessary skills to impact people positively. By now, you can think of your "why" for helping those in need. Be completely authentic to your goals and aspirations.

Inspire Others

Sheikh Ahmad Deedat, the greatest debater of his time was tested in the last nine years of his life with a stroke that left him paralyzed from the neck down. He was known for his energy, productivity, and intelligence yet, during these nine years he was not able to even speak a word. But his faith remained strong despite what he had experienced. Even Christian missionaries who traveled from all over the world were not able to convert him to Christianity, but instead they were inspired by him. Through his eye movements, he was able to communicate and invite people to Islam. He continued to do his favorite thing in life, reading, as his family members would hold the newspapers and books for him to read every morning. It was his desire to still keep learning and growing that kept him going until the last day of his life. He could've rested and waited for the angel of death, but that was not an option for the Sheikh. Now, how many of us were inspired by these nine years of Sheik Deedat's life?

Did you observe with that story as an example, that physical limitations are no hindrance to some people? If their hearts are filled with the intent to inspire and teach others, then nothing can stop them from achieving this. You too, could become a source of inspiration if you are willing to fight the darkness of any pain you may experience in life.

Inspire the world

You're not here in this world forever. There will come a time when your time will be up. The question would be if you made an impact in your lifetime or you will be forever forgotten?

It is not the number of people that you've inspired. This is not a competition to see who had inspired the most people. The focus should be more on the quality of values that you've taught and shared.

Share it to the world before going to the grave. Have good intentions with it and avoid having a hidden agenda with helping others. If you have a clear vision and a good intention then you will have an extra boost to keep going. You will not have the guilt that you're pretending to be someone that you're not.

I know that all of us don't have the same journeys, goals, and struggles. Having unique experiences could be a puzzle to those that never have gone through it. You could make them empathize with you by narrating your life stories. This will make them think that the world is indeed larger and shift their focus to their miseries and egos, then find some solutions to cope with their issues.

Besides helping them, you are helping yourself forge those values. You will be constantly re-evaluating your past, present, and future. You could also create bonds and connections with others that are genuine and could help you with their knowledge and experience. Another benefit is you will realize the diversity of each person's life.

Inspire Others

You would bring out the humanity of the people that you've inspired and hopefully they will also teach those around them. This is the best aspect of guiding and helping others. It's like a chain effect that goes on and on. Spreading encouragement of sharing good values that would alleviate one's suffering.

> *"The Prophet PBUH said to Ali Ibn Abi Talib RA 'By Allah, if a single person is guided by Allah through you, it will be better for you than a whole lot of red camels.'"*
> Al Bukhari & Muslim - Riyad as-Salihin 1379

And by the way, did I already tell you that I have abandoned my wheelchair? That's right. Even though I am still limping and many parts of my legs and toes are numb, but Alhamdulilah, Allah SWT has listened to my prayers and granted me back the ability of walking on my feet without any aids. So have faith in Him, and get back up on your feet.

FINAL WORD...

There's no end to any journey. That's why, the final word within my book is going to remind us all of what we need to DO and forget about whatever else that will block our ways from the main purpose of why we were created. i.e., to be devoted to God Almighty and to worship Him until we breathe our last.

> *"And We already know that your breast is constrained by what they say. So exalt [Allah] with praise of your Lord and be of those who prostrate [to Him]. And worship your Lord until there comes to you the certainty (death)."*
> Qur'an 15:97-99

A few points to take away from the above beautiful verse:

1. Allah SWT knows what you are going through. But despite this fact,
2. Glorify Him as much as you can. Through your faith, hard work, remembrance, and knowledge.

3. Prostrate and humble yourself before God and call upon Him repeatedly. Never give up on your supplications, and finally,
4. Worship Him alone, without any partner, until the end. Worship doesn't only mean prayers, fasting and the like, but rather, every good action with pure intention can be considered as worship. So, this is our job until the end . . .

Now, it is time to look into other challenges that may come my way and face them with the exact might, courage, and fearless heart which was the result of facing the previous challenge.

Stay strong.
Wael Ibrahim

ABOUT THE AUTHOR

Wael Ibrahim is the founder of the Aware Academy, a platform dedicated to help those who are struggling with pornography consumption. He is the author of several books, namely *CHANGE: A motivational system to break free from undesirable habits*, especially pornography. *Beat it: 50 plus shades of hope*, *AWARE: find out who you are without porn* and *Better Me: 365 ways to transform your everyday life*.

Wael Ibrahim is a certified Master life coach and currently is the student counsellor of the Australian Islamic College in Perth, Australia.

www.ingramcontent.com/pod-product-compliance
Lightning Source LLC
Chambersburg PA
CBHW021438080526
44588CB00009B/587